The man who painted in Welsh

Sir Kyffin Williams, RA, Wales's greatest painter

by Ian Skidmore

The definitive biography, told through conversations with the artist and his friends.

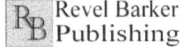

Revel Barker Publishing

First published by Seren Books in 2008.
This, revised and re-edited, edition published by Revel Barker Publishing in 2011.

Author's royalties from this, and all of Ian Skidmore's books, go to *Help The Heroes* and *Combat Stress* charities.

ISBN 978-1-907841-04-0

Cover portrait by Peter Edwards: *Sir Kyffin Williams in his Studio, seated in front of his painting 'Waterfall, Cwmorthin' June 3-4 2003;* Oil on canvas
Tabernacle Collection, MOMA WALES, Machynlleth.
Reproduced by kind permission of the artist.

Published by Revel Barker
revelbarker@gmail.com
66 Florence Road
BRIGHTON
BN1 6DJ
United Kingdom

Author Ian Skidmore can trace his ancestry back a thousand years to Ralph the Knight who built castles along the Welsh border, and two of his books, *Owain Glyndwr* (about another ancestor) and *Gwynedd*, the biography of a county, became required reading for degrees at the University of Wales, but he was dropped as a broadcaster by BBC Radio Wales on the grounds that he sounded 'too English'.

A former soldier, printer, news editor, freelance journalist and TV presenter, he has written 30 books, 26 of them about Wales, without assistance from the Welsh Arts Council but – with the support of Sir Kyffin Williams and the Marquess of Anglesey – aided by the Royal Literary Fund which awarded him a pension in recognition of his 'services to Welsh culture'.

His autobiography, *Forgive Us Our Press Passes*, was voted BBC Book Of The Year, had the highest listening figures on Radio Four, and was read twice on the BBC Overseas Service. The *Daily Post* described him as 'Wales's funniest columnist'.

He is married to award-winning author Celia Lucas and now lives in retirement in Cambridgeshire.

In fondest memory of Kyffin.
And to Celia, who entertained many of the contributors
to this biography, while they entertained us with stories of
a great artist, our friend.

Preface to revised edition

Nearly two decades have passed since, at Kyffin's request, I started on his biography. It was a suggestion he made at a convivial dinner with my wife Celia and me at our home, Aberbraint, Llanfairpwyll, Ynys Môn. To my great joy he went on to suggest that after future dinner parties I should tape record his reminiscences, and interview a number of his many friends. Alas, he did not like the result because of the revelations about his family. We agreed that I would not publish it during his lifetime, and I hoped that meant that I would never publish it. A world without Kyffin would be a very much poorer place and I was not sure I wanted to be part of it.

The project, however, continued to fascinate him. Indeed he subsequently sent over to my house anyone he thought might add to it, including his cousin. I thought, in fairness, that when I finished the book he ought to see it. He read it, suggested some alterations and sent it back with one of his most delightful cartoons which showed him in hunting gear on horseback and the caption *Thank you for the Memoirs of Kyffin*.

People who knew him well were aware that he rejoiced in such perversity. On his 80th birthday, our mutual friend and landlord the Marquess of Anglesey hosted a celebration at Plas Newydd to which the great and the good – most of them Kyffin's good friends – were invited.

The only guest who planned not to turn up was Kyffin. He had decided that he did not want a celebration. As the time of the party drew near, I had an anguished telephone call from the Marchioness, who instructed me, 'He is your friend, get him here.'

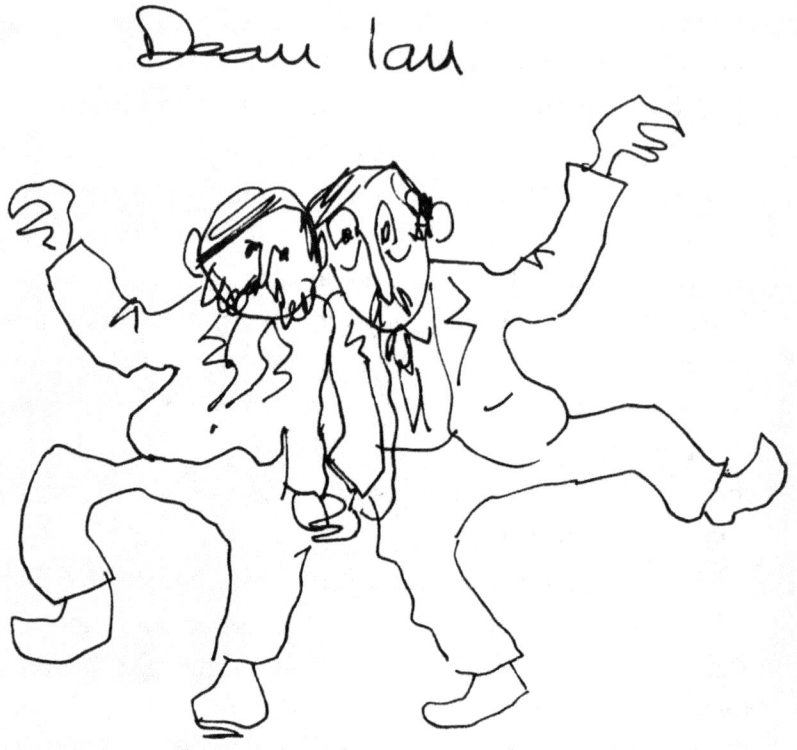

Dear Ian

I tried, but in the end it was his great friend Annwen Carey-Evans who persuaded him by driving to his house on the Straits and ordering him into the car. Needless to say, he was the life and soul of the gathering and his speech had them rolling in the aisles.

It is not so much his paintings I will remember and cherish. It is his gift of laughter which he shared so generously with any company that was lucky enough to have him among its number.

He had so many facets that writing his biography was akin to writing the biography of the 8th Army.

The gentlest of men, his secret ambition was to be a soldier. He was the archetypal Welshman and an almost cartoon version of the English public schoolboy. He railed against the Welsh art establishment, yet secretly longed to be accepted by it.

If there is a heaven, which Kyffin doubted, then it will echo to the sound of his laughter. Neglected by the art establishment in life, in death everyone wanted his works.

It is ironic that within days of Kyffin's death, Wales's policy makers were facing conflicting views on where he should be remembered. Artist Andrew Vicari called on the assembly government to secure as many of Kyffin's works for the nation as possible. He said Sir Kyffin should have a permanent exhibition at the National Museum in Cardiff, or even a purpose-built gallery in the Welsh capital. Anglesey Council leader Gareth Winston Roberts called on politicians and prominent figures in the art world to back Anglesey's plans for a dedicated gallery on the island. 'Anglesey is the obvious choice for a gallery dedicated to the work of local artist Sir Kyffin Williams.' he said.

Kyffin had already given 400 paintings and drawings to Oriel Ynys Môn, to be displayed at a planned £1.5m new gallery. Culture Minister Alun Pugh said the assembly government supported the Anglesey project but acknowledged there were different views on the issue.

Alun Gruffydd, Anglesey Council's principal museums and culture officer, was in no doubt: 'We were fortunate enough to have had Sir Kyffin Williams as an advocate for the arts on Anglesey and he was an active supporter of our work at Oriel Môn since we opened over 15 years ago.'

Kyffin would have loved it.

He was a stern president of the Royal Cambrian Society of Art, which he once left in disgust. The kindest of men, he was passionate about blood sports. He was an invalid who outlived most of his healthier contemporaries. An intensely private man, he loved public speaking, at which he was a master.

He was a writer of genius: his book *Across the Straits* is a minor Welsh classic. A shy man, he was nonetheless a brilliant self publicist. The first Welshman to become a Royal Academician, his gifts as a landscape painter and portraitist assure his place in the front rank of British contemporary painters, yet he would splutter with rage at any mention of much of contemporary art.

Though I said of him that he painted in Welsh, and a Welsh proverb defines a Welsh house as having a harp in the corner and a Kyffin on the wall, he spent the greater part of his adult life in England. His critics complained he only became a Welshman in middle age when he ceased to be called John and asked to be called Kyffin.

He could laugh at himself. As *The Times* obituarist noted: 'He was an unassuming man, only too happy for an oil he was painting to be inadvertently improved by its toppling, face down, on to his new tweed hat, or for the texture of a watercolour, being tackled *al fresco* on the windy shore of Llanddwyn, to be helped along by the addition of wind-blown sand.'

He was generous with his work. After a stay or a dinner party his hosts would receive a cartoon and perhaps a verse, for he was a brilliant cartoonist.

He was a *bon viveur*, yet aggressively teetotal. Fired only by fruit juice, he was a brilliant conversationalist; his anecdotes were tinged with imagination and made iridescent with fantasy. No connoisseur of food, he loved dinner parties.

A very wealthy man, he spent little on himself. In desperation, his Cardiff agent Mary Yapp, shocked by his threadbare, paint-stained wardrobe, regularly bought him suits.

I had a private parlour game in which I tried to sum him up in a word. The word I finally chose was lovable. Yet there was, as I was to find, a better word.

Although he spent little on himself, his purse was always open to his friends. Many were the secret contributions he made to people and to charities.

I have personal proof of his generosity. When my English accent became unacceptable and I was dropped by BBC Wales, I also lost my column in the *Daily Post*. Without an income I fell on hard times.

As Kyffin was my closest friend, I confided in him my distress at losing the two outlets that defined me and my worries about making ends meet. I told him I was going to have to sell my library, my antiques and my collection of Welsh paintings, including an early landscape oil and a drawing he had given me. Out of the blue he sent me a letter:

> Dear Ian,
> You certainly have a predicament and I feel that I can help.
> If you like I will give you the current price for your oil of Cribyn Goch which is £6,000 and the big black and white drawing which is £1,500.
> Let me know.
> Love to you both,
> Kyffin

He rescued me by buying back the gift he had given me. With the Marquess of Anglesey, he secured me a pension from the Royal Literary Fund for my 'contribution to Welsh Culture'. Curiously the Welsh Arts Council refused me a bursary for every one of the 27 books I have written celebrating that culture. On consideration, perhaps the best word to define Kyffin – and one I suspect he would relish:

Friend.

This is a 'revised' and 're-edited' edition because the original version contained an inordinate number of misprints – what we in the trade call typos or literals – presumably because the publishers printed the early roughly-typed first draft of a submitted manuscript without benefit of editing, correcting, proofreading and even, it would appear, without any reading whatsoever within the publishing house.

It was so badly typed that one of the very few reviews it received concentrated almost solely on the misspellings within it and drew attention to the fact that the publishers were also the imprint of Poetry Wales Press and operated with assistance from the Welsh Books Council. A corrected version was promised by the original publishing house but never transpired. Hence this new revised and re-edited edition.

Ian Skidmore
March, Cambridgeshire.

Dear Ian and Celia
many thanks for
the Memoirs
of →

Chapter one

Kyffin Williams painted in Welsh. It could hardly be other. Though he was the product of an English public school, Shrewsbury; soldiered in Northern Ireland, an unlikely officer in the Royal Welch Fusiliers; studied art at the Slade, evacuated then to wartime Oxford; and taught art in London, at Highgate School, his antecedents nevertheless form a chain of Welsh gold that glitters down the centuries.

The pious, the profane, piratical even. Soldiers and scholars and the downright outrageous are numbered among his ancestors. His is less a genealogy than a novel by a Celtic Fielding. All coming together in the complex conundrum that was Wales's greatest living painter and for many years the country's only Royal Academician.

He was heavy with honours. An OBE, Deputy Lieutenant of Gwynedd, MA, D Litt, Fellow of three Welsh colleges, president of the Royal Cambrian Academy; only the second artist to receive the medal of the Society of Cymrodorion since its inception in 1880. In the New Year Honours of 1999 he was knighted.

Not a bad record for a man who, according to a school report, 'is incapable of lucid thought' and who believed, with some justice, he had never been fully acknowledged by the arts establishment of Wales. It is also true – and astonishing – that his work was never in his lifetime chosen for any exhibition of Welsh art that had gone overseas. A friend told how he overheard two pillars of the arts establishment agreeing that Kyffin was the greatest single threat to Welsh art.

Yet the picture-buying public venerated him.

Tall, an action man even in his eighties, with a scholar's stoop, dressed in tweeds as ancient as his lineage, he was the sum of a mass of contrasts. For most of his life he was John Williams. Indeed, you could place his friends in context by those who called him John and the later ones to whom he will always be Kyffin. It is a measure of the man that his biographer, though struggling to be impartial, cannot bring himself to identify him by his surname.

His voice, outlook, his foxhunting, mountain-walking way of life were unashamedly élite, unreconstructed *uchelwyr*, the dwindling race of Welsh squires. Yet his paintings, drawings and prints push at the frontiers of art. More than one perceptive scholar has likened him to Van Gogh, with whom he shared a lifetime's thrall to epilepsy and diabetes. They differ in one important respect. Van Gogh did not sell a picture during his lifetime. Kyffin's pictures sold as fast as his dealers could hang them.

Since 1997, on the night before the opening of his London summer exhibition at the Thackeray Gallery off Kensington Square, potential customers slept on the street. A queue master was always appointed to decide which picture a customer should have. At the 1998 exhibition Kyffin was distressed that many were allowed to buy two, which meant that people at the tail end of the queue went home empty handed.

His Cardiff agent Mary Yapp took a call from a man who was worried he could not get down the night before the opening of Kyffin's 1998 exhibition at her Albany gallery. He offered £100 to anyone who would stand in for him.

The owners of the three galleries where he exhibited (the

third was the Tegfryn in Menai Bridge, Anglesey) claimed that no other Welsh artists, and few other British artists, have had such an eager public. Interestingly, all three gallery owners are women and all of them acted as surrogate elder sisters to the unworldly Kyffin.

His output was staggering. No picture took him longer than a day to paint and he painted on most days.

He was a source of joy and happiness to his friends, wildly generous and deeply caring, with a photographic memory that was an album of outrageous anecdote. Yet he claimed never to have known happiness and to have lived most of his life on the dangerous frontier of suicide. A frontier his much loved and admired elder brother Richard crossed.

Chapter two

Kyffin came to art by accident, and reluctantly, on the advice of a doctor who in discussing his epilepsy told him he was abnormal. The doctor insisted that on no account should he return to his pre-war occupation as a land agent which would involve sitting examinations. He advised taking up painting, an occupation that would not tax his brain.

Kyffin had been drawing since the age of two. The subject of his first sketch was his brother Richard sitting on the chamber pot. It earned him a merciless beating with a tortoiseshell hairbrush from his prudish mother for being a dirty boy.

Understandably, therefore, he did not want to become a painter and was very upset at the thought of being abnormal. An Irish nursing sister consoled him. 'Don't worry about that,' she advised. 'Sure, ninety per cent of the world is abnormal.'

It was his sense of humour, and a monumental awareness of the absurd, that saved him. As to being abnormal, there is a country saying that insists you cannot breed tame rabbits from wild ones and eccentricity did not merely run in Kyffin's line; it danced in high glee.

A distant ancestor, a squire of Gogerddan near Aberystwyth named Sir George Pryse, thought if there could be Owen Owens, William Williams and John Johns, then why not a Pryse Pryse? He ordered his infant son to be so christened.

Unfortunately, the officiating vicar was deaf. Given the

name the first time, he said, 'I am afraid I cannot quite hear you.' 'Pryse,' repeated the child's mother. 'I am afraid I cannot quite hear you,' said the vicar again. 'Pryse,' repeated the child's mother more loudly. Three times.

'I am afraid I cannot quite...'

This was too much for the choleric squire. Standing in his manorial pew, he shouted, 'Pryse, you bloody fool. PRYSE! PRYSE! PRYSE!'

This time the vicar heard. 'I christen this child Pryse Pryse Pryse Pryse,' he said firmly.

'And so it was,' Kyffin always added, building one absurdity onto another, 'until the poor boy died in consequence of having been bitten by a fox. He was hunting the family's own pack of hounds when a fox went to earth. Pryse Pryse Pryse Pryse went after him and the fox bit him.'

He was at home with all manner and condition of men but his happiest memories were of the farmers of his childhood. He would listen entranced to their stories. Men like Huw Jones of Swtan (Church Bay) on Anglesey who told him one day of a bottle that had been found in the chimney of a nearby farm. In it, he said, had been found a very old piece of paper with four prophesies written on it.

'The first,' he said, 'was that a time would come when people would go up in the air and fly like birds. And that has come true, hasn't it?' he said. The young Kyffin agreed it had.

'The second was that people would go down to the bottom of the sea and swim like fish. And that has come true, hasn't it?' Once again the young Kyffin agreed.

'And there would come a time when people would talk to each other across continents. And they do, don't they?'

18

Again Kyffin agreed.

'And the fourth was the date of the end of the world,' said Huw Jones, and his voice grew heavy with apprehension. Alarmed, Kyffin leaned forward and asked, 'When will that be?'

Farmer Jones looked out of his window and a long silence ensued. At last he turned. 'Damn,' he said, 'I've forgotten.'

A childhood friend, Olwen Caradoc Evans, remembered Kyffin as a lonely little boy who was always accompanied on his roams round the countryside by his Jack Russell terrier Bonzo, an out-draft from the Tanatside Hunt. But Olwen also remembered him as the fittest little boy who could run up and down a mountain with ease.

Kyffin's oldest friend was the landowner and founder of the country's largest private forestry business, Roger Williams-Ellis of Glasfryn, on the Llyn Peninsula. His first memory of Kyffin concerned his childhood skill at drawing.

'I was seven and had been invited to a party at Plas Gwyn which had been taken by the Williamses. We were handed a series of twenty or thirty drawings by Kyffin, who was about 12, and asked to identify the objects. They must have been well drawn because one was a fountain pen and you had to identify its make.'

Seminal to Kyffin's development as an artist was a pack of foxhounds, the Ynysfor, a small private foot pack of six couple. The country they hunted included some of the most glorious mountain scenery in Britain and was certainly the roughest upland hunting. Over Eryri (Snowdonia), across Crib Goch, up and down Tryfan and all over the formidable Glyders the followers ran in pursuit of the hounds.

The importance of the Ynysfor Hunt and its members in Kyffin's life cannot be overstated. No one painted mountains better than Kyffin and he has said that everything he knew about mountains he learnt out hunting with that pack of hounds. Through the Ynysfor he also met the man who gave him his first lessons in painting.

In time, and to his intense surprise, painting became more important than staying up with the hounds. Enchanted by the panorama in the high mountains, he would let the pack run on and stay behind to capture the picture they made.

Ynysfor gave Kyffin not only his artist's eye: it gave him a family. Rebuffed by his own mother, he gloried in this new improbable family in their house above the kennels. A house that until Maddocks built his embankment at Porthmadog in the 19th century had been part of a large island, Ynys Mawr.

Ynys Mawr was a wooded mound a mile long and a quarter of a mile wide with little bays and cliffs. It was one of the many small islands in a stretch of Wales which until the sea was turned away must have been among the most beautiful bays in Europe. Even now, the prospect from Maddocks's embankment to Cnicht mountain, shaped like a Norman helmet, and Eryri beyond, is breathtaking and leaves one wishing that Maddocks had left well alone.

The Joneses of Ynysfor were among the last of the true northern Welsh squirearchy whose family hunted their own hounds. They had farmed and lived off their own land for a hundred and fifty years. Not aristocratic. Organic, rather. A family that spoke Welsh on the hearth, an old

Welsh long forgotten that had forty words for dung heap.

The first Jones to come to Ynysfor, more than two centuries ago, was the son of a Welsh parson. Jackie Jones went to Oxford to read theology but had instead spent his time hunting. He brought to his new home the first pack of rough-coated black and tan Welsh hounds. The Hendy, in which he lived, like all old Welsh houses had no view. Beauty in Wales is more often received through the ear rather than the eye. The Hendy was a long low house with a stepped gable into which a small dovecote had been built. It overlooked a stable yard and hound kennel. It sheltered below the hill peak from the brisk Snowdonia weather. It had been built with stones that probably came from a Romano-British fort on the crest.

In 1865, Jackie's grandson John built a new house on rising ground facing the peak of the Cnicht, a substantial house with a good sized hall and well windowed rooms. His son, Colonel Evan Jones, was a darkly handsome soft-spoken man, known to the girls as 'Sentimental Evan'. He was master of the hounds and when he hunted always wore the hunt uniform of brown tweed jacket and breeches with blue facings and a blue velvet waistcoat.

In contrast, there was nothing sentimental about his brother, Captain Jack, who found his girls among the rough and ready country girls in the Maentwrog pub where he drank at nights.

Between the brothers were eight sisters. All but one died unmarried. The sweethearts of the other seven were all killed in the First World War, a tragedy no less poignant for being common among girls of their age. Kyffin and Roger were regular visitors.

Sixty years on Kyffin remembered those days. Strange

tales were told about the Hunt in the wild mountains. The strangest can be found in the transactions of the Honourable Society of Cwmrodorion. In the 1890s when Captain Jones's grandfather had the hounds, the pack picked up an odd scent on the slopes of Moel-y-Gest. They found in a moss-covered hollow – but it wasn't a fox. Concealed in the moss and bracken was a man, gaunt and thin, clutching a bible and a milk bottle.

The followers took him down to Porthmadog where he was identified as a sea captain, the victim of religious mania, who had made a hermitage there. His lonely life and near starvation had done him little harm. He was soon well enough to go back to sea.

The Joneses' ancestral home on the banks of the River Glaslyn was, like most Welsh farmhouses, constructed to let in as little light as possible. The walls were covered in fox brushes and masks, portraits of earlier masters, paintings and photographs of hounds and terriers, including a portrait of the legendary terrier Juno, first in a long line that goes on to this day.

It was a very democratic hunt. As well as the 'gentlemen', the followers included farmers and local youths. They had to be fit, for the Ynysfor country consisted of miles of upland wilderness. Its followers had to scramble through bracken, over rough scree, round marshy hollows and up stiff mountain climbs. A twenty-mile day was not unusual.

Captain Jack Jones succeeded his brother Colonel Edward Bowen Jones, who carried the horn as both huntsman and master for the first forty years of the twentieth century. Captain Jack had served in the First World War as a company commander in the Royal Welch

Fusiliers. His men in D company were mostly recruited locally and in later years he helped many of his soldiers.

He was not a gregarious man, except with his own kind. An outsider – which meant anyone from another district – he described as a 'sinister English person', whatever his nationality. On days when the field was, in his view, too large, he lost no time in shaking off the majority.

He carried his service revolver in the field, and when one day a shepherd said of a bedraggled fox, 'If I'd had a gun I would have shot it,' Jones replied: 'If you had, I would have shot you.'

His language was hair-raising. The mountains rang to his cry of 'Sod you, hounds! God damn and blast the whole bloody pack!'

One distinguished follower of the Ynysfor Hounds was the author Patrick O'Brian, at the time a penniless author living in a cottage in Cwm Croesor. His unsurpassed novels of the British navy during the Napoleonic wars were still in the future. But when he came to write them he had not forgotten his days on the mountain.

O'Brian's stepson is Count Nikolai Tolstoy. In his biography of his stepfather, Tolstoy wrote: 'The genesis of Jack Aubrey can be found in Jack Jones, a possibly unique figure of unqualified admiration in Patrick's (O'Brian's) life.'

O'Brian drew on Captain Jones, according to Tolstoy, earlier in his literary career when he 'unmistakably drew on Captain Jones' qualities of leadership in his portrait of the historical commodore. He appeared to be made of iron and oak, quite unchanging except that he grew a little more affable as things grew even worse.'

Kyffin recalled his Ynysfor days:

The Ynysfor family were remarkable. My family had known them for a hell of a long time. I started going out with them when I was about 13 or 14. The Jones sisters joined us on the hunt. They were pretty tough. One of them, Minnie, had hunted hounds herself during the First World War. They used to position themselves on hilltops across the country. The hounds would find and one sister on her peak would shout to the next sister, 'Have you seen the hounds?' and that would be relayed to the next sister on her hillock maybe a mile away. And so on until the final sister who might shout, 'Gone into the Cwm!' and 'Cwwwwwm' would echo over miles of countryside. That is how it used to be done. Now it's all done by walkie-talkie.

My companions were Roger, Ernest Naish, who was a lieutenant in the navy, Cedric Maby, who was in the Foreign Office, and Harry Glyn, one of the Glyns of Hawarden, the family into which the Gladstones married. He was very tall, about 6ft 6ins. He always said that if he was killed he wanted a stone carved on the summit of Cnicht. In fact he was killed at the first battle of Narvik.

Except for Roger who was younger than I was, they were all just a little bit older. Very few local Welsh boys went out. It might have been some strange social thing but hunting doesn't seem to be part of the Welsh set up, though the Ynysfors were completely Welsh and of the land.

When I first went out hunting I couldn't keep up with Ernest Naish who had very long legs. It was really heavy going because Jack Jones was a terrific walker. An incredible man. Precipices meant nothing to him. I once saw him take hounds across the vertical face of the Craig Ddu in the Cwm Llan above Gwynant in order to drive a fox from a narrow ledge.

They had a kennel huntsman, Frank Edwards, who lived in Cwm Bychan and walked every hunting day ten miles over the mountains to the meet. He would walk and run another twenty to thirty miles out hunting and then in the evening walk home in the dark over the mountains. He was a lovely man.

There was one wonderful old huntsman, Harry Jones, who was always known as Harry Bet. Bet was his mother who had been a maid in the Goat Hotel in Beddgelert. The story was that Gladstone was staying there. Gladstone and Bet had an assignation and Harry was the result. Certainly Harry was an immensely distinguished man and he looked rather like Gladstone. Everyone looked up to him. There was another huntsman called Evan Go, the blacksmith. He had one eye.

I was always a very nervous boy and kept very much in the background. I was a loner, too. My brother Richard was keen on team games but I was happiest wandering the fields with my dog Bonzo and a gun.

My brother was too kind for blood sports. He came with me rook shooting and was appalled when he shot one. I had to finish it off. There was something about hunting and the knowledge of hounds that appealed to me. I was fascinated by the way hounds found the scent of a fox and stuck to it. Magnificent! The great thing is patience. You cannot be impatient and Jack, though he was a very exuberant sort of person, was immensely patient with hounds. If you try to lead hounds they will let you, and that is fatal when you are on foot in the mountains. The hounds must always hunt themselves because often they are far, far away.

I learnt a lot from Jack. Not only about hunting. About the birds and the wild life. About the majestic silences and the mountains themselves. The weather and clouds which could suddenly clear to show you a precipice beneath your feet that you did not know was there.

Hunting also kept me terribly fit. Sometimes I would end up on the side of Snowdon about four o' clock in the afternoon and I would have to walk back almost to Pwllheli, to Abererch, which would be about twenty miles. If you are fit and harden yourself when you are young it really does pay off in later life. The reason I am fit at eighty is that when I was a boy I hunted in all weathers, trying to keep up with the hounds. As I walked, I watched. I noted in my mind the shapes of clouds above me and below. I saw the sun bursting onto the grassy breasts of the hills as it broke through the clouds, creating glittering explosions of light that raced across the valleys and hills. The movements of the clouds as they swept over the mountains, dragging great shadows behind them, began to fascinate me. And as I watched, the knowledge that would later be useful to me as a painter I stored, subconsciously, in my head.

When I did begin to paint it came second to hunting. One day in February 1947 the hounds were meeting. I had taken a couple of canvases with me and I started painting about nine o'clock in the morning up in the mountains and waited for the hounds to arrive. I could see them at the meet in the distance but I went on painting. In that moment I realised that creativity took preference over destruction. After that, painting always took first place.

In August later that year I was staying in a little pub called Gernant at the foot of Cadair Idris. Although I had been at the Slade I did not know I was a painter, really. I took two canvases and sketchbooks and climbed up to Llyn y Gadair, which is just under the summit, and painted an oil. I pegged it and with a canvas on my back I climbed up the Fox's Path to the top of Cadair, went over the summit and did some drawings of Llyn Cau on the other side. I came back to the top, climbed down the Fox's Path and painted another picture at the bottom and pegged it again. Those were the first two paintings that made me think I might have a future as a painter. I don't know that I thought they were good but they did make me think I might be a painter and not a schoolmaster.

Roger Williams-Ellis recalled: 'Colonel Evan had died by the time I went there but four of the sisters still lived with Jack and another lived nearby in Llanystumdwy. She was considered very superior because she had been out to France as a governess and could speak French fluently…

In the house there was Minnie, the public figure, the magistrate, who called her car Jane Austen; Sybil, who used to snap questions at you; Miggsie, and poor little Annie who did all the chores. What little gossip they didn't know wasn't worth knowing. The house was littered with fox skins, paws and masks. No electricity, just oil lamps.

The hunting country was mountainous but John (Kyffin) was very fleet of foot. He had this ability to leap from rock to rock. You had to be tough to follow hounds at all. The weather was usually dreadful. Sleet you couldn't see through or driving rain.

Didn't worry us. When we were hungry we would get behind a wall and eat a sandwich. Then from John's back pocket out would come a small pad. Rain or snow meant nothing. He drew whatever was in front of him, whatever the weather.

The pack knew every inch of the mountains. Once they found their way into Llanfrothen church during a service. A churchwarden crept to the pulpit where the parson was in mid-sermon. 'The Ynysfor hounds is in the church,' he whispered. 'Then show them to the Ynysfor pew,' replied the cleric, who had a fine sense of the obligation due to landed proprietors.

Minnie Jones always had an ear for a tale. It was she who told of visiting a tenant and hearing her call her dog forty different names, every one of which meant dung heap. She told Kyffin of a meeting with the water bailiff in Llanfrothen:

'Oh Miss Minnie,' he said, 'the other day I was in Cwm Croesor and I see something up the road. And I say to myself, well, damn, is that a man or a bullock? And I look closer and, *Duw,* it's neither. It's Mr Clough Williams-Ellis.'

Clough Williams-Ellis was the architect who later designed the Italianate village of Portmeirion and became Sir Clough Williams-Ellis.

The house was a magnet to Kyffin. In summer after hunting was over he shot crows and pigeons, helped to bring in the hay and listened enraptured to the stories the family told as they sat in a semi-circle round the drawing room fire.

Captain Jack told of the day he was swimming in the deep junction pool of the Glasfryn and the Ynysfor rivers when a police sergeant came to search for a farmer who had disappeared.

Years later an elderly man called Hansen, recently retired from the Indian police, came to Kyffin for lessons in watercolour painting. Over lunch he said he had been tracing his Danish ancestors among the Skagerrak and Kattegatt islands where they had lived. On one island, where nearly everyone shared his name, the harbour master sent for the only islander who spoke English. An

English overlaid by a strong Welsh accent. Though the two got on well, it was only when Hansen was about to leave that, very reluctantly, the Welshman told his story.

'More than twenty years ago I was farming in the Glaslyn Valley in Caernarfonshire,' he said. 'One day Megan my wife came back from Porthmadog market with a bright yellow scarf in her basket. 'Look, Ifan,' she said, 'I've bought this to go to chapel on Sunday.' Damn it, it was an awful thing, so I told her straight: 'Megan, if you wear that thing for chapel I'll go away and never come back.'

'Well, you know what women are like. What does she do but go off to chapel the next Sunday with the scarf round her neck. Come the next Sunday and there she was going out of the house with the damn thing round her neck again. Defying me she was. A man must have his pride. I watched her till she went through the gate. Then I packed a bag and went to Porthmadog where a schooner was loading a cargo of slates. She brought me here and I am bloody not going back.'

Another eager follower of the Ynysfor Hounds and one of the most remarkable men in Wales was Ernest Naish, who at 88 still ran three farms, at Cwm Pennant, Trawsfynydd and on Anglesey. He was huntsman to the pack for most of the twelve years he followed it.

He was a man of many talents. When he joined the pre-war navy he was a dagger man, one of the fast track naval élite. This enabled him to claim the naval record for going on courses: ten years. Alas, the day he joined his first ship he went for a typhoid inoculation, was jabbed with a dirty needle and became seriously ill.

Back ashore, he commanded a trials party that inspected

submarines on maiden voyages. He was about to board one when he was taken ill again. The submarine was *HMS Thetis*. 'My successor is buried in Holyhead,' he said. 'A very painful thought that is with me all the time.'

Invalided out, Naish bought an Anglesey sheep farm and weaving mill, though he knew nothing about either trade. 'I just asked my neighbour what to do next,' he said. Good neighbours, obviously. He became an international authority on sheep and wove tweed of such beauty it was taken up by fashion houses in London and Paris. The war intervened. When he came back, the tweed market had been wiped out by an eighty per cent purchase tax.

Fortunately he found a part-time job to boost his farm income. He set up and ran the Ty Croes Guided Missiles Station at RAF Valley, commanding fifteen jet fighters and a staff of a hundred. In his spare time.

He remembered it being great fun: 'I would do the morning milking, then fly down to the Air Show at Farnborough, say. Then fly back in time for the evening milking.'

The Air Ministry asked him to go to Woomera in Australia to report on a new pilotless plane. He barely had time to buy his second farm from a small advert in *The Guardian*: 'Five hundred-acre farm on Cwm Pennant, with cottages and fine Victorian villa, built by wealthy father of quarry owner. £4,500.' He only had time to look at it from the road and he bought it the same day.

The bard asks: 'Oh Lord, why did you make Cwm Pennant so lovely and the life of a shepherd so short?' In the matter of age, Naish made a liar out of the bard but he agreed with the sentiment: 'I am part of this farm,' he said 'just like the pigs and the sheep. This is the worst land in the Cwm, a foot of peat on rock. It is a hard place to make a living but my heart is here. In forty years I have spent only four nights away. That is why I have a hobby that keeps me at home.'

The hobby was painting. Although self taught, he was acknowledged to be a very fine painter by the few people he allowed to see his work. Perhaps his main claim to fame, though, was that he taught Kyffin to paint. Naish would not exhibit. He did once and regretted it immediately.

'Kyffin twisted my arm to take part in this touring exhibition sponsored by the Countryside Commission,' he told me. 'I put four or five paintings in. He valued them at £500 a piece and I thought, that's fine, they are safe, no one will pay that. Blow me if I didn't sell two. I made a resolution never to do a silly thing like that again.'

That was some years ago but you could tell it still hurt.

'I am a non-profit-making water-colourist because, frankly, I don't need the money,' he continued. 'I paint purely for my own pleasure. I get an idea by walking round the farm and looking at things, then I come back and ruin a lot of old envelopes sketching on them. I cannot start painting until the picture is complete in my head. I start in one corner and work across the paper. I don't know any of the rules. Never had a lesson. Don't know why I paint and why I paint such big pictures. It is very exacting. It takes hours and hours. My eyes and my limbs are going so I can only manage twenty minutes at a time.'

This multi-talented shepherd also designed a water-driven Aga in which an electric heater was powered from a generator he built and in turn was fed from his stream. Another invention was a machine that extracted heat from cold air.

As he said, 'Nothing really. Just reverse the principle of the fridge.'

He followed hounds for more than forty years. He took a break from sheep shearing to talk to me about his long friendship with Kyffin:

> I discovered the Ynysfor pack when I was 19. Captain Jack was a funny withdrawn sort of man. Gruff and surly with a huge handlebar moustache. When he saw I was obsessed with the way hounds work, he took me under his wing. I was certainly obsessed. My brother, who was also in the navy, bought a motorbike in China for £2. He did it up and sold it to me for £8 and I often rode it all the way up from Plymouth for a day's hunting with the Ynysfor. Jack liked me for that. I also got on well with Minnie. She was the shining star amongst them, the one with personality. On the day of her death she was to have had a picnic with my family. We could not believe it when we were rung up to be told she had died over her breakfast.
>
> She loved telling stories. We were talking about broken Welsh and she said she had the greatest difficulty keeping a straight face when she asked a local person about a relative who had tuberculosis. '*Duw*, Miss Minnie,' the person said, 'we do be very worried. She's dropping fat.'
>
> I first met John (Kyffin) when he was 12 and his mother brought him to a meet at Ynysfor. He was younger than I was but we quickly discovered we shared this obsession with the way hounds were. From then on we were inseparable. He won a prize at school for art but he refused to take an art book. There was a book on the scenting of hounds, which was an account of some very interesting work a man had done in this field. Quite

rightly, he insisted that was what he wanted. Lent me the book. Very interesting it was too.

The Ynysfor didn't attract a large field. Usually there was Captain Jack, another naval chap Harry Glyn, Cedric Maby, John, Roger and me. One day John invited me to the Royal Welch Fusiliers' St David's Day dinner and to stay over with his family at Abererch. The next day was a Sunday and John suggested that we go out and I could show him how to paint. We duly went out, I pulled out my paper and paints and showed him how to do it. Fifty years later he acknowledged my contribution in a speech at a dinner. He remembered that I had told him how colours change. Burnt Sienna and ultramarine blue mixed together make grey. That was the first lesson and he quoted it.

We shared one memorable moment. People say foxes are terrified of the hounds but I remember I was out with Kyffin on Garn Madryn on Llyn. We saw two foxes coming up towards us, stopping occasionally to sit and listen to the hounds in the next field. Not a bit worried. Completely in control of their environment.

Look here, there are only three things animals are interested in and they all begin with F. Feeding, fighting and I leave you to guess what the third 'f' is. It certainly isn't fear.'

The third surviving member of the companions of Ynysfor was Cedric Maby who was to have a distinguished career as a diplomat. He was captured by the Japanese and interned in Peking before being sent to Turkey where he became vice-consul at the embassy in Istanbul in 1942.

He was in Istanbul during the period that Cicero, the valet of the ambassador Sir Hugh Knatchbull-Hugesson and a German master spy, stole Britain's secrets from the embassy safe. Secrets so important that the Germans did not believe them and paid Cicero in counterfeit money.

In Peking he became an authority on classical China. When he retired to Wales he translated a thousand years of Chinese poetry into Welsh which was published as *The Red Cockerel*. He and his wife, the daughter of the Swedish ambassador to Turkey, were fervent Welsh Nationalists.

He recalled for me the pre-war hunt fortnight of the Anglesey Harriers, hunting every day and dining and dancing in the Bulkeley Hotel in Beaumaris every evening. It was from this energetic orgy that the custom began, of throwing shovelfuls of hot pennies to the crowds in the streets.

Ynysfor hangers-on wanted to know why we couldn't have a ball like the people in Anglesey. Captain Jack was against it and regular followers agreed with him. But Colonel Evan seized every opportunity to wear the dashing hunt uniform with its red tailcoat and blue facings and so a ball was planned.

We booked the Oakley Arms at Maentwrog, which has the most elegant ballroom, and applied to the magistrates for an extension. To our amazement, it was turned down. Minnie was furious. She was a magistrate too, of course. She got into Jane Austen and drove off to give the licensing magistrate the rough edge of her tongue. He was terribly apologetic. 'Oh Miss Minnie,' he said, 'I didn't realise they was church hounds; I thought they was chapel hounds. That's why I turned them down.'

The decision was reversed but the magistrate was taking no chances. As closing time approached the village policeman arrived on his bicycle. Captain Jack didn't really approve of balls and he had spent most of the evening in the public bar with his cronies. He spotted the policeman and offered him a drink.

I have two memories of that ball. Minnie and Clough Williams-Ellis opening the ball with the most spirited Viennese waltz you have ever seen – and the policeman riding his bicycle in circles on the Oakley car park with an expression on his face of utter bliss.

Kyffin remembers the ball. His partner was the granddaughter of Lloyd George. 'I was obsessed with the girl,' he told me. 'I was terribly susceptible as a young man.' And he admitted that, at eighty, he still was.

Captain Jack was to die tragically in 1948 while hunting with his hounds. A fox went to ground in a rocky earth above the bridge at Penmaenpool, near Dolgellau. A farmer warned him the rocks were unsafe but Jack ignored the warning. Seconds later he was pinned under falling rocks and killed. The estate and the hounds passed to a soldier nephew, Edmund Roach.

He was a difficult, sulky man. In the bad winter of 1974 when even the tractors were frozen, Roach had a row with his kennel man Robert about a job that had not been done. Robert said he would have done it if he hadn't had to spend so much time with the hounds. In a fit of anger, Roach stormed off to the kennels and shot twelve hounds. The young entry he gave away. It was the end of the Ynysfor Hunt.

The Eryri Hounds, with which Kyffin still hunted regularly until his death, were founded by a neighbouring landowner and friend of Edmund Roach, Pyrs Williams of Hafod Llan. Williams's family had been tenant farmers on the Hafod-y-llan and Gelli Iago estates at Nant Gwynant since the 17th century. The estates comprised a large area of Snowdonia and included the peaks of Snowdon (Yr Wyddfa), Lliwedd and Cnicht. Williams bought them and in a stroke became the biggest and most powerful landowner in the mountains.

Williams and Roach were hunting in the Lake District when Roach was offered two couple of hounds by the Windermere Foot Harriers. He turned them down because they were too small. Williams took them to hunt hare on another farm he owned on Anglesey. Then he started hunting foxes in the Ynysfor country. This made Roach furious. He abandoned the slopes of Snowdon, owned and farmed by Williams, and the two men never spoke again. Occasionally the two hunts met. On such occasions, Roach left his hounds with Naish to bring home and drove off in his land rover with darkened brow.

Williams's estate included the ruins of Brynkir Hall, Garndolbenmaen. In the early part of the nineteenth century Brynkir had been bought by a family named Huddard. A kindly family, Kyffin remembered:

> They found work for unemployed tenants building roads and cottages on the estate. Indeed, it became a family tradition that when an heir inherited he got local men to build another room onto the house. Presumably from the same charitable motives, the family also built Brynkir tower, a wonderful folly on a hill, ideal for a Rapunzel to let down her hair, and recently restored by Prys's grandson, the present master of the hounds Richard Williams, and his wife Frances, a descendant of Beatrix Potter.

> The Huddard estate came up for sale when a

gambling Huddard lost all the family money. It is said he was so obsessed he would bet on two snails racing across a chessboard. Things became so bad and the creditors so demanding that one morning he and his family vanished, leaving the breakfast things unwashed on the table, and the house gradually fell into ruin.

Wendy Wynn Williams was one of the few girls allowed to follow the Ynysfor Hounds. Her ancestors were Williams Wynn until one of them started a money lending business in Chester which became Williams Bank. With an Anglesey man, the same ancestor also developed the vast Dorothea slate quarry. He changed his name because he thought himself grander than the Williams Wynns.

The quarry owners were hard task masters. At the time of the Irish potato famine starving families came over looking for work. Wendy's great grandfather would employ them only if they changed their religion and became non-conformists. She recalled that a lot of the workers were related to the family: 'I remember walking round with my grandfather and people saying, Morning, cousin. My grandmother snootily referred to them as Welsh cousins. The workers were not badly paid. Many of them invested in the shipping firms the quarries owned. They all had a plot of land, a cow, chickens and a pig, a small holding run by the wife. But they were only paid when they could work. No pay if they were rained off. There is an eight-mile wall round the Vaynol Estate. No wages for the local men who built it. They were paid in bags of corn.'

At 74 and married to Lt Col Roy Davies, a fellow subaltern of Kyffin's in the Royal Welch Fusiliers, she recalled there were conditions to hunting with the Ynsyfor. 'I was not allowed to speak,' she said. 'Captain Jack hated chatter. Very few girls went out. I was honoured but I had to be like a boy. No rubbish like being helped over a stile. Ten mile points.

> I remember the teenage John Kyffin, terribly thin and spindly, pale complexion and huge ears sticking out. He looked like a silver birch. He was a terribly nice boy with a terrific sense of humour. But terribly shy. He was a special favourite with the Ynysfor. All the other boys were 'That Boy'. He was the only one Captain Jack called by his name.
>
> After hunting we would troop back to Ynysfor for a boiled egg tea. Followers had an egg each. Only John was a two egg man. An honour he shared with Colonel Evan and Captain Jack. The family loved him. They reckoned his mother didn't look after him.
>
> To help Kyffin, they commissioned him to paint Captain Jack's portrait. Everyone was very keen except Captain Jack. He made Kyffin muck out three huts before he would sit for him. The portrait is still at Ynysfor, though I have never seen it exhibited.
>
> The Ynysfors were out of this world. They belonged to old Wales. They still carried on the ancient tradition of Welsh hospitality. Any house of any distinction kept open house. My grandfather remembered there was always a pan of *cawl* (soup) on the kitchen fire. Any traveller who called was given a bowl.
>
> He also remembered their mother who kept to the old way of eating. The main meal of the day was at lunchtime and in the evening she had only a bowl of buttermilk. Even when they had smart dinner parties old Mrs Jones would insist on her bowl of *llaeth enwyn*.

The hounds were not over fed. There was one story you never dared repeat in front of the Captain. A kennel huntsman must have gone into the hounds late one night. In the morning all that was left of him was his boots.

Miss Minnie was the worldly one of the sisters. She had been to America to show the Americans how to hunt foxes. She had several boyfriends. One who doted on her was a local curate who once came to tea on a hot day. He sat down at the table and said, 'I sweat something awful.' That was the end of him.

They were a great power in the land and it did not do to cross them. The bench in Porthmadog consisted of Colonel Evan, Captain Jack and Miss Minnie. A lady of ill repute was giving evidence. Miss Minnie said, 'She's guilty', and couldn't be persuaded she was only a witness and could not be punished. They also had somebody who was a terrible poacher. No question of a court appearance for him. Colonel Evan and Captain Jack caught him and threw him in the river.

Miss Sybil wore flighty hats. She would appear at a tea party in a bright pink hat with a veil whereas the other sisters wore sensible, woolly hats.

Miss Miggs was the homely one who boiled the eggs. They had little maids from the village who were terrified of anyone who spoke English. They were frightened of taking stuff into the dining room and they used to try to get me to take it in for them. Captain Jack was larger than life. I remember once I was sitting on the bonnet of a Lagonda car and we drove into Llanfrothen with some boys inside and others hanging on the running board. There was a pub in Llanfrothen and, as we passed, out through the window came a man. It was Captain Jack, moustache bristling. 'What are you doing with that scum?' he roared. 'Get back home, girl!'

Staying at Ynysfor was quite an experience. It was lit by oil lamps. The paintwork was dark brown and hanging over the banisters was a huge rug of fox-skin and there were masks all round the house. It was a jewel. You had all these other families around which were new money. The Ynysfors weren't. They were only slightly anglicised. They all spoke Welsh on the hearth.

I wasn't old enough to go to the hunt ball but there was a terrible to-do. You daren't mention it to Captain Jack. He insisted he wasn't going.

It was Great Aunt Cecily who first called Colonel Evan Sentimental Evan. She almost got him into terrible trouble. The Anglesey hunt fortnight was a great time. There had been a real steeple chase; literally from steeple to steeple. That ended when two people were killed. The Anglesey hunt ball was the great climax. It was held in the old Bulkeley Assembly Rooms, which had a balcony round the ballroom. Great Aunt Cecily was up on the balcony and Colonel Evan was below with his arm round a girl. Cecily dropped a piece of ice cream down this girl's front and she screamed her head off. Everyone thought Colonel Evan had done something he shouldn't. But Lady Bulkeley had seen what happened and told on her.

Another girl who was an occasional hunt follower was Kyffin's only living blood relation, his cousin Betty Mewies. She would come every year from her home in Stretford, near Manchester, for a fortnight's holiday with the Williamses at Plas Gwyn, near Criccieth. She told me:

I met John Kyffin and his brother Dick for the first time when I was 12 and fell passionately in love with them both. I think there is nothing unusual in that. There is a great affinity with first cousins and, besides, they were both in their different ways so eminently lovable. Dick was the more glamorous. He was tall and darkly handsome; he smoked Passing Cloud and wore a cravat. John Kyffin was small and frail. He was known as Little John. He showed me great instinctive kindness. It was unusual because he was fifteen and at that age boys do not want girls of twelve hanging round. He used to take me out walking and taught me a lot about birds. He would shoot rabbits but he loved birds. I remember once he rescued a small owl with a broken wing and he was so gentle. He carried it home and nursed it back to health in a games room at the rear of the house. I say I loved him. I should have said everyone loved him. Even my mother who found fault with everyone could find none in Kyffin.

We used to holiday in Anglesey. We would all be on the beach. Dick and Little John used to swim. Dick, a big strong lad, used to come out of the water and Aunt Essyllt, his mother, used to wrap him in a huge towel and rub him briskly the minute he stepped on dry land. When Little John came out of the water he was ignored and that sums up the way their family worked. Dick was never allowed to clear a table or wash up: Little John and I had to.

There was another side to John Kyffin which he kept very quiet about. His music. He cannot read a note but we used to go to the pictures at Porthmadog. If it was a musical he would come and sit at the piano afterwards and play the pieces note perfect. Dick had lessons but Kyffin played entirely by ear.

I used to hunt at Ynysfor. Aunt Essyllt, who was one of the first women drivers, used to take us to the meet in her car. One day smoke began to pour out of the engine. It was me who had to go to a nearby farm for a bucket of water while the boys sat in the car.

41

We used to hunt in all sorts of weather. I had mixed feelings about hunting. When the fox passed me I didn't always tell anyone and I hated it when the fox went to ground and the terriers were sent in. But the farmers insisted on it. Ynysfor wasn't a recreation. It was a pest exterminator.

Chapter three

The Byzantine complexities of Kyffin's pedigree were unravelled in his autobiography *Across the Straits*, an account of a Welsh world now sadly lost. When it was first published in 1973 the book caused a furore among the deeply class conscious Gwynedd society whose antics it recorded with great glee.

Across the Straits was republished in 1998 so it is only necessary to summarise an ancestry that sometimes seems more a library of plots for scandalous historical novels than a family tree. A tree that includes King Philip IV (Philip the Fair) of France and, via his daughter, Edward I, the king who conquered Wales with an army of 15,000, nine thousand of whom were South Walians.

Kyffin also descended from Edward II's favourite Sir Hywel y Pedolau (Howell of the Horseshoes), the giant son of the king's nurse who flamboyantly broke horseshoes in battle to discomfort enemies.

The first recorded non-giant, non-royal male ancestor, born in 1666, was Wmffre ap William John ap Rhys, who came from yeoman stock and was village blacksmith in the Anglesey hamlet of Llansadwrn. According to a local legend, he had tethered a difficult horse to a tree stump outside his smithy. The horse pulled out the stump and beneath its roots ap Rhys found a pot of gold. The truth was rather more prosaic. When he was 20, Wymffre married Catherine Meredydd, an 88-year-old heiress. With her dowry he bought a farm, endowed alms houses and instituted charities.

He then anglicised his name to Humphrey Williams.

His family were the issue of a second wife Margaret Prydderch. His son Owen bought Treffos, the manor house of the parish, where the family was to live until a descendant sold it a hundred and fifty years later in 1904.

A roadman told Kyffin the story of a young Mr Williams of Treffos and the snake: 'They sent him away to school in England and he came home with a snake,' he said. 'And an old 'ooman in the village said if Mr Williams keeps that snake he is dead, just like that. Well, what did they do? They sent him to South Africa. Years later young Mr Williams came back from South Africa. He was walking across the field in front of the house. And he tread on this thing in the ground and something went into his foot. And do you know what it was? It was skeleton of the snake. And the bone went into young Mr Williams' foot and he got blood poisoning and dead, just like that. The old 'ooman was right.'

Treffos was famous, as many Anglesey gardens are, for its rhododendrons. On a bus once going past the house Kyffin heard two old women talking. 'Oh, look at those lovely hydendrons,' said one. The other said, 'Don't be so silly they are not hydendrons, they are rhodydandoms.'

Owen had two sons. One, John, became chaplain to Princess Augusta of Wales and held three livings on Anglesey. In the ancient courtroom of the nearby town of Beaumaris there is a plaster cast in the magistrates' retiring room. It shows one farmer tugging the tail of a cow, another its horns, while sitting at his ease a solicitor milks it – a visual description of the career of Owen's other son Thomas who bought the family's second Anglesey manor Craig y Don.

A country solicitor, he managed to represent both sides in a dispute over the ownership of the mineral rights of Parys Mountain, one of the most valuable copper sites in Britain. By the time it was settled in 1785 Thomas controlled the mine while his clients had become sleeping partners.

He produced his own coinage, 250 tons of pennies and 50 tons of halfpennies, some designed by a Coventry jeweller Francis Skidmore. This money, which the miners could spend in company stores, shows a druid's head encircled by a wreath bearing 24 acorns, the Parys Mountain company logo and the legend 'Success to the Anglesey Miners'. Thomas hoped the issue would lead to a contract to produce British crown coinage. It did not, largely because he fell out with Prime Minister Pitt. He controlled the whole of the British copper industry, becoming in the process a millionaire, an MP and founder of the Williams Chester and North Wales Bank. His bank became the nucleus of the Midland and the vast industrial empire he built was the nucleus of ICI.

He was not the archetypal capitalist grinding the faces of the poor. His nickname among his miners was Tom *Chwarae Teg*, Tom Fair Play.

Thomas's descendants mainly concerned themselves with spending rather than making fortunes. One grandson, Owen, commanded the Royal Horse Guards. The other, Hwfa, built Sandown Park racecourse and became a director of the Savoy, Claridge's, the Berkeley and Simpson's in the Strand.

Through Owen, the brothers and their six beautiful sisters had the entrée to the Marlborough House set, over which the future Edward VII genially presided. As a result all the sisters, including Edith, the most wayward, found aristocratic husbands. Edith, who drove a four-in-hand of ostriches, became one of the legion of Edward's mistresses while at the same time dallying with the Marquess of Blandford. This caused both the Prince of Wales and Hwfa to challenge the marquess to a duel. On neither occasion was a shot fired but Hwfa was subsequently injured in the leg when a demented post office clerk wildly fired a revolver at him in The Mall.

Marriage caused much greater damage. Hwfa's bride was a fortune hunter, Florence Farquarson, who moved to Paris after he died and succeeded in spending his last penny a few days before her own death. She wrote a book called *It Was Such Fun*. That title, and Queen Victoria's remark 'The Williamses are a bad family' seem to sum up that branch of the family.

Meanwhile, the royal chaplain Owen's branch of the family, from which Kyffin descends, was irredeemably good. It continued to pour out a succession of worthy clergymen, twenty-seven in all, every one a country parson, who over two hundred years occupied nearly every living on the north western coast of Anglesey.

Kyffin's family was also connected to Sir William Vincent of Bangor, who in the 1920s was the permanent head of the Indian civil service, represented India at the League of Nations and was the architect of the sub-continent's independence in 1948.

His great grandmother Frances was a painter who also studied astronomy and had a passionate interest in shipping. Indeed, she was said to have charted the Menai Straits before she was twenty-one. Her husband James held the parish of Llanfairynghornwy, on Anglesey, an area

46

with a coastline of dangerous reefs where ships were frequently wrecked. On March 26, 1823, the day they came back from their honeymoon, a packet boat *The Alert* struck West Mouse rock and broke up. Out of 140 people on board only seven survived. James and Frances could only watch in horror as the others drowned: they had no boat sufficiently well found to broach the angry seas.

They determined to buy one. James dunned the local gentry for subscriptions; Frances made lithographs of a painting she had done when George IV made his only visit to Anglesey. Their Anglesey Lifeboat Service was founded before the RNLI, which took it over in 1856. The rescue boat was based at Cemlyn Bay below his rectory. James coxed it and Frances often joined his crew of farmers to nurse injured survivors.

Together they saved 400 lives and James won the first RNLI gold medal for bravery to come to Wales. Ironically, he won it not in the boat but on horseback. On March 7, 1835, the *SS Active*, a Belfast cargo boat, was wrecked in breakers so high the rescue boat could not be launched. James leaped on his horse and swam it out to sea to throw a grappling iron into the *Active's* bowsprit rigging, saving the crew of five.

If Kyffin Williams inherited his painting gifts from his great grandmother, his impish sense of humour comes from her son, his grandfather Owen, a country clergyman and, like his father, a chancellor of Bangor Cathedral, incidentally the highest office the family achieved.

A parishioner of Kyffin's grandfather told him: 'He was telling me of the time when he was hit in the eye by a ball at school. How they was to take him to hospital, take his eye out and put it on a plate in front of him, and how he could see as well with his eye on the plate as he could with it in his head.'

Owen was infected with his parents' passion for lifeboats. His first parish, Boduan, was in the centre of the Llyn Peninsula which enabled him to cox lifeboats on both coasts.

One of his relatives recalled how she was being driven by Owen in a gig. At the foot of the hill on which the rectory stood the pony halted and refused to budge. 'Maggie Jones,' called Owen, 'send out the pig!' The cottage door opened and out shot a small pig which bolted up the hill, closely followed by the pony. They arrived safely at the rectory door.

Two of the parson's sons, James and John (the latter was Betty Mewies' father), went to sea and fought for revolutionaries in Chile. Kyffin recalled:

> John, who was always known in the village as Mr Johnny, was small and freckled and totally without fear. If ever a horse had to be broken they sent for Mr Johnny. He went out with my Uncle James to Chile in 1880 to fight for the revolutionaries against Spain. James stayed out there and became a captain in the Chilean navy.
>
> Bob, as he was also known, came back married to an awful woman, Josephine, the daughter of an Antwerp harbour master, who was all sorts of hell wrapped up. He sent a joking word to the rectory that he was coming back with his bride and she was foreign. To the locals that meant she was black. The word got out. Mr Johnny has married a black woman.
>
> I once went to see an old lady in Llanfairynghornwy. She was about 90 and I had never seen her before. To my astonishment she got up and threw her arms about me,

kissing me passionately. I realised she thought I was Uncle Bob. He had gone to sea and used to put in at Liverpool where she was in service.

Betty Mewies told me: 'We found out later that he was venerated by the Chileans and is to this day, as far as I know. He was a very adventurous person. John Kyffin loved him. Kyffin looked exactly like his father (Harry, the youngest son). Both he and his father were very gentle, unlike my father.'

Kyffin was very aware of his family and his position in it. 'My family lost all its money and ceased to be county,' he recalled. 'I am the end of the line, the inverted peak of a very large triangle. I have illegitimate relations on Anglesey but I am sworn to secrecy.'

His great uncle Tom Kyffin was rector of the Anglesey parish of Llanbadrig, the patron of which was Lord Stanley of Alderley, a Mohammedan. Through the Bishop of Bangor, the Reverend Tom asked Stanley to restore the church and another at nearby Bodewryd. He agreed, provided they would be restored in an Islamic manner. There is abstract glass behind the altar and Islamic tiles.

This same Lord Stanley had golden retrievers, of which he was very proud. Two of Kyffin's needy aunts, Annie and Mamie, heard that if anyone praised the colour of his animals he would always say: 'Do you really think it a lovely colour? May I give you a length of tweed in the same colour?' It worked for the aunts, too.

Kyffin told me:

His funeral was bizarre. He was succeeded by a Roman Catholic priest. As the coffin was lowered, the new Lord Stanley took off his top hat, only to be kicked by his brother. 'Not your hat, you bloody fool, it's your shoes you remove.'

This Lord Stanley was said to have a Spanish gypsy mistress whom he kept in Elen's Tower on the cliffs at South Stack, Holyhead.

My father's cousin Guy Williams had an exotic connection. He was a general in charge of recruiting in the Far East. On a visit to Tonga he threw a party for Queen Salote's husband, who became so drunk he keeled over and died. Uncle Guy had to break the news to the queen. He insisted that telling the queen he had killed the king was the bravest thing he had ever done.

My great grandfather was impressed by a poor boy who was a teacher at Rhosybol. He got my mother's grandfather to teach him Greek and Latin and eventually he got him into Jesus College, Oxford. His name was John Rhys and he became the first Professor of Celtic Studies and Principal of Jesus. Famously, when a suggestion was mooted that baths should be installed at Jesus, it was Professor Rhys who said: 'What, may I ask you, is the point? They are only up here for eight weeks.'

The Reverend Owen's youngest son Harry, Kyffin's father, was considered too delicate to work; indeed he only went to school briefly, in Southport, on the Lancashire coast. He became a wood carver until he decided to make a career in banking, about which he knew nothing. He joined the North and South Wales Bank which had taken over the family operation. He was given a revolver and a terrier and told to open a branch at Penydarren, in the then lawless Rhondda.

Harry Williams was a tall, handsome man with a nature so lovable that the locals took to him at once. He was the antithesis of the traditional bank manager. He trusted everyone. He played the organ in the church and as a gesture of appreciation to the people of Penydarren, he carved a lovely reredos over the altar.

From the Rhondda he moved as a clerk to Midland Bank branches in Porthmadog, Caernarfon and finally to Llangefni, back home on the Isle of Anglesey.

Late in life he married Essyllt Mary, the daughter of another vicar from the adjoining parish. Where Harry was outgoing, she was withdrawn. Her mother had been a chronic invalid, prey to migraine attacks, and had spent much of her life in a dark room, her head swathed in brown paper. After her mother's death, Essyllt's girlhood was spent with her gloomy father whom she worshipped. When she was sent to bed she would creep out onto the landing to look at him adoringly as he smoked unaware below. He seemed incapable of feeling. His diary entry for July 1, 1883, reads: 'Showery. Little girl born at 12.30 pm.'

He sent the desperately insecure small girl to boarding school in London, where she was so lonely she ran away, and thereafter was educated by a stream of governesses who served only to repress her further. Unwillingly, and paralysed with shyness, she played hostess at parish teas. At one such tea party a farmer told an improper story which gave her the unshakeable view that Welshmen were vulgar. She forbade anyone ever after to speak Welsh in her presence. Her revulsion to the language extended to her name. 'Esyllt' is the Welsh form of 'Iseult'. Her father gave her the name because he was reading about Esyllt in the Mabinogion when she was born. It was a name she hated but her father insisted that if she weren't to be known by her Welsh name he would call her 'Polly', which she

thought vulgar. Kyffin always spelt it with a double 's',
Essyllt.

Although related to leading Anglesey families, she was
treated as a poor relation by them. Her relatives, the Rice
Roberts, lived in some state in a fine house called Rhiwlas,
but the children were never allowed to visit Essyllt at her
rectory home which their mother considered low. At family
dances she was never allowed to sleep in the big house. A
bed was found for her in a nearby cottage.

By the time of her marriage at the age of 34, Essyllt was a
mass of inhibitions. In the mechanics of marriage and
motherhood she excelled. She was a fine cook and a careful
housekeeper. She was desperate to do the right thing yet
incapable of showing affection. Kyffin, the younger son,
cannot remember ever being kissed or cuddled by her.
Never having known love, she was incapable of showing it.
As though she realised this, she attempted to make up by
being over protective, especially of her elder son Richard.

Many years later when they were well into their forties,
Kyffin suggested that Richard, by now ill and the frail
bubble of his self esteem irrevocably punctured, should
take a holiday abroad. His mother was horrified. A trip
abroad, his first, would have put him beyond her
protection. It did not happen.

Said Kyffin:

> My mother suffered from a very deep inferiority
> complex. When we inherited the house on Anglesey we
> were ostracised. Her cousin, who was disinherited, was
> part of the hunting set on Anglesey and all the hunting
> people took her side against my mother. They were
> utterly beastly to my mother. They refused to call on her
> at all.

One of them, Claire Daniel, who used to push me in my pram when I was a baby, came up to me when I talked about the ostracism in my book and said: 'You were quite right to mention it. I am totally ashamed of myself.'

In contrast, my father got on with everyone. Although my mother was emotional, she never showed it. She never showed any interest in my painting. When I had my first exhibition in London in 1948, she came up, saw it, but was not impressed. She would never compliment me. She went round it without saying a word. She couldn't show her feelings. When my father died in 1941 she didn't seem to be concerned at all.

Wendy Davies thought of her as fey. 'She was not a caring mother, the Ynysfor family thought. She did not feed Kyffin, which is why he always got two eggs, I suppose.'

Ernie Naish remembered Essyllt: 'She was an odd woman. She didn't want to be a Welsh person, she wanted to be English and look down on the Welsh. His father was the reverse. He was never happier than when he was nattering away in Welsh. She was small and unimpressive. Very correct and standoffish. Never happier than when she was talking about the old landed families of Anglesey. Though, I must say, she was always very decent to me.'

Roger Williams-Ellis recalled: 'His father was jovial but I always found his mother depressing. She never understood why he wanted to paint and never had a good word for him. She concentrated on Dick who had a very unhappy life. He wasn't allowed to marry the girl he wanted. Her parents were against the match.'

Betty Mewies had happier memories:

Aunt Essyllt was very kind to me. I think she was a woman born before her time. She was a very clever woman, deeply frustrated. Had she gone to university there was no telling what she might have accomplished. She was a very efficient woman, a wonderful organiser. I remember she used to give coffee mornings for the church, long before anyone had heard of coffee mornings. She started the Hospital Linen Fund where people gave a penny a week to provide blankets for the local cottage hospital. I have always understood that Aunt Essyllt's Linen Fund was the precursor of the Hospital Saturday Fund with its penny a week subscription.

She was a stickler for etiquette, I remember. She told me that it was wrong at a dinner to wait for the hostess before you began to eat. No hostess wants her guests to let their dinners go cold.

It was always Kyffin, never Richard, who did the family chores. It might be supposed that this favouritism would have affected the brothers' relationship. Not so. Kyffin was always so sweet, so loving and so kind.

Kyffin recalled: 'I knew I was the second child and my brother was number one. He was brilliant at everything. I knew he was better than I was so I was never jealous. I couldn't resent him because from the moment I became conscious I knew he was better. I was told so by my mother but it was unarguable. When I scrambled my way into Shrewsbury he was a bit of a swell. In both cricket and soccer teams. He was terribly, terribly good to me. We got on extremely well. I remember once I hit him because he wouldn't play with me. All he did was look at me with his large eyes and I felt an absolute shit. He was extremely kind but hopelessly over sensitive.'

Later, it was Kyffin who became the dominant brother as Richard slipped into alcoholism and obsessive gambling.

Outwardly he did well. At school he was captain of rugby, a first class footballer and cricketer. He excelled at fives and running; he was house monitor, top of the modern sixth and destined for an Oxbridge scholarship.

But as Kyffin explained, it all went wrong:

> I didn't know of his tragedy for thirty years and then he told me. Shrewsbury had a system of fagging called douling from *doulos* the Greek for slave. Until boys had been at the school for two years they were called douls. If a monitor wanted something doing he opened his study door and shouted: 'Doul!' The last boy to arrive did the dirty work. Dick thought he heard a shout and ran to a monitor's door. The monitor said, 'What do you want, funny face?'
>
> That was the moment my brother's life was destroyed. Something hit him hard. After a year he thought he had a very funny face, after two years he believed he was so repulsive no one wanted to look at him. He was very good looking but it so affected him he could not function. He couldn't ask for rooms anywhere. If the landlady said she was full up he believed the real reason was because he was so repulsive. I had to look for rooms for him. If someone crossed the street it was because they did not want to look at his face. It's a known medical condition, I believe.
>
> He refused to try for an Oxford scholarship. Our school reports are with the Bangor archivist. You can see the masters were puzzled by Dick. He did go to Jesus College but not on a scholarship. He did no work at all. He spent his whole time in sport and idled his way through a course in modern languages. He was to go into

the Indian civil service but he only managed a third. He went into a solicitor's office in Pwllheli until the war when he joined the Royal Welch as a private soldier. I was an officer and we used to have clandestine meetings. He later got a commission but it was another tragedy. He was sent on a battle school course. The instructors were throwing plastic hand grenades. One landed in a gorse bush and blew his leg off. It didn't worry him all that much because he knew he was revolting. This was merely underlining it. Not only was his face revolting, he only had one leg. I had to tell my mother and I do not think she ever got over it.

After the war, Dick worked as a solicitor for Walker, Smith and Way in Chester, where he was much loved by everyone who knew him, including this biographer. His erudition and fusillades of Latin tags demolished many a prosecutor. He was affable enough, but one always felt he had built a wall round himself it would be impossible to breach. It was heart-rending to see his lonely figure stumping into the magistrates' court in the town hall. Eventually, he retired to Anglesey where Kyffin protected him from everything but the spectres in his own mind until he gave up the struggle and died.

Kyffin recalled: 'Twice, I think, he tried to kill himself. When he was 40 he went to live in an old folks' home. When it closed, a colleague, Dennis Diamond, found him rooms in a pub in Rossett. He became an alcoholic and took an overdose of pills but he recovered. Dennis found him more rooms but he was getting more and more depressed and every night he went to bed hoping he wouldn't wake up.

'He came back to Anglesey but things went from bad to

worse. One day I gave him a lift to Beaumaris. He said in a very firm voice, "Goodbye." The next day his landlady rang to tell me he had been found dead.'

Despite his 27 family clerics, Kyffin was always a non-believer. But he had one thing in common with them. They were never happier than when talking about the oddities of their flock, whom they visited tirelessly.

Kyffin's 'parish' included old family retainers like Nanny Williams Fingar, so called because she lived in Llansadwrn near the signpost. A tough little body and a passionate supporter of Manchester United, she preferred being called Nanny Williams Verney. She was a terrible snob and that was the name of the baronet she had worked for. She was horrified when her sister died and was buried on the side of the church path where the ordinary people were interred and not on the other side with the *Pobl Mawr*.

Once when Kyffin visited her he was startled to be asked: 'Do you ever see that Kyffin Williams fellow?' He said he did. Why? 'Will you give him a message from me? Will you say him damn and blast?' Kyffin asked what for. 'Because he never comes to see me.'

Kyffin had more reason to feel neglected than Nanny Fingar. When he was born on Ascension Day 1918 in Tanygraig, a small house on the outskirts of Llangefni, on Anglesey, his mother immediately put him out to be fostered by a neighbouring farmer's wife. He was brought back to Tanygraig only to attend his christening, performed in a local church by his 87-year-old grandfather, who two years earlier had christened his brother Richard. They were the only services he ever performed in English, presumably out of deference to his daughter-in-law.

Promotion took the family to Chirk, in Denbighshire, where Harry Williams became manager of the Midland Bank. There the boys had a succession of nurses, who were warned if they ever spoke Welsh they would be instantly dismissed. One had a more terrible gift to impart. All his life Kyffin believed it was her cruelty that led to his epilepsy.

Outward appearances were more important in the Williams family than inner torment. Kyffin's father had always limped. The family were told that this was the result of an accident. His nurse had been taking him out in the pram when a herd of horses rushed by and knocked the pram into a ditch. Harry, it was said, broke his leg but the nurse was so frightened of admitting he had been in an accident she told no one and the leg healed itself awry.

Kyffin told the story in *Across the Straits*. Among his readers was the chief surgeon of the Orthopaedic Hospital in Oswestry, founded, incidentally, by a Williams cousin, Agnes Hunt. He subsequently visited Kyffin at his home in Pwllfanogl on the Menai Strait and asked him to imitate the way his father walked. Kyffin did. 'As I suspected,' the surgeon said, 'it's all rubbish about your father having an accident. He had a congenital abnormality of his hip. It was supposed when he was young to be disgraceful and a dishonour to the family. Obviously a story was made up to account for it.'

Three years after he was appointed to Chirk, Harry Williams broke his other leg in a fall, his health deteriorated and he retired. By this time Essyllt had inherited Brynhyfryd, a furnished house near Beaumaris in its own landscaped grounds. Unfortunately, the aunt Letty Pritchard, who left it to her, left nothing to her already wealthy daughter. The daughter Mary Pritchard Rayner went to law, and although the judge decided in Essyllt's favour, he ruled that each side should pay its own costs. The sum involved was well beyond the means of Kyffin's parents. The house was sold and the family moved to a rented home in south Caernarfonshire.

Wendy Davies believed the issue was a fine Rockingham tea service which was much prized in the family. 'Law suits are definitely a pastime on Anglesey and Mary Pritchard Rayner sued Mr and Mrs Williams for the tea service. It would have been more sensible to have given her the tea service but Mrs Williams chose to defend and lost everything. Anglesey is very cliquey and ostracism was complete. She was not a very balanced person and that must have had a terrible affect on her.'

There is, perhaps, a further more bizarre explanation of his mother's hurt. Coyly to some, more explicitly to others, Kyffin would say he was the natural son of his mother's contemporary, Sir Richard Williams Bulkeley. An elderly local journalist claimed that in his youth he had been told the story of Mrs Williams' *mésalliance*. Kyffin himself admitted it to this biographer. What was puzzling about this was the physical resemblance of Kyffin to his mother's husband. Brother Richard, on the other hand, resembled no one in the family.

The next home of the Williams family was an ugly, castellated house near the north eastern shores of Cardigan Bay, now a hotel. It is surrounded by the most glorious landscapes in Britain. As Kyffin often said, 'It was here I began to assemble, unknowingly, a vast library of feelings, sensations and knowledge that were to form the foundations of my future life as a landscape painter.'

With the move to south Caernarfonshire began what Kyffin insisted was the happiest time of his life. He and his brother were sent to board at Tre-Arddur House school, a forbidding collection of buildings on a rocky hill above the beach on Holy Island, an island that includes Holyhead and which is joined to mainland Anglesey by a causeway and a bridge.

Iorwerth Owen Williams, the school's proprietor, was a small, dark, vivid man from an old Anglesey family, married to a kindly English woman. There was a wonderful atmosphere at the school where Kyffin spent his seventh birthday.

The master who taught Kyffin art at Tre-Arddur was F H Glazebrook, a remarkable and inspirational man who lived for while in a tent on Llanddwyn beach and wrote the definitive guide book to Anglesey and the North Wales coast. He was a superb sailor and charted and published *Pilotage of the Menai Strait.* A master of perspective, it was Glazebrook who crystallised Kyffin's lifelong devotion to drawing as the basis of all visual art.

Kyffin won his first prize at Tre-Arddur. Not for painting but for poetry. He was in quarantine with chicken pox and the pupils were asked to write a poem about the snow outside. His was judged the best.

As so often in Kyffin's life, disaster was waiting in the wings. In 1929 he and Richard had their tonsils taken out. Richard recovered quickly but Kyffin was far from well. In the middle of his operation the surgeon had a heart attack during which, in a frenzied sweep of his scalpel, he not only removed Kyffin's tonsils and adenoids; he took out the uvula and soft palate as well. The family were not told of the accident. The hospital blamed his slow recovery on natural frailty. His parents found out the truth in the oddest way.

It was the custom in those days for a relation of a patient to call on the surgeon's wife. Kyffin's Aunt Mamie called. In order to get to the front door of the surgeon's home in Upper Bangor, she had to go through the conservatory, where she saw a pair of boots among the geraniums. It was the surgeon. A second heart attack had killed him. Poor Aunt Mamie had to go to the door and when the surgeon's wife answered it say, 'I am frightfully sorry but your husband is dead amongst the geraniums.'

Before the operation, Kyffin had been a bright pupil and was being groomed as a future head of school. Afterwards he was unable to concentrate. Brother Richard easily won his scholarship to Shrewsbury. Not only was there no question of Kyffin achieving this: there were doubts he would even pass his Common Entrance examination.

Friends tried to help. He was doing the algebra paper with the vicar of Holyhead, the Reverend Rowlands, as invigilator. 'Having trouble, my boy?' the vicar asked. 'Let's go through it together.' The vicar did the whole paper. When the results came Kyffin had passed in every subject except algebra.

When he got to Shrewsbury School – the smallest boy there – he discovered that the boys who did best in examinations sat at the back of the class. Kyffin sat at the front. It was some time before he realised they sat there because it made cheating easier. Kyffin with his Welsh church upbringing could not bring himself to be dishonest. All the way through the lower school he was, in consequence, given up by his masters as hopeless.

Eventually it was decided that he would leapfrog two classes and move to the upper school where he could be coached for his school certificate. His new form master, John Key, objected. He told the headmaster Kyffin was so stupid he refused to be responsible for getting him through the school certificate. Happily, Kyffin was taken on by David Bevan, the best master at the school. Bevan was a confident, quiet, kindly person. His teaching was so good that when Kyffin took his school certificate he got more credits than any other boy in the school. He had dreaded the science and physics papers. Fortunately, the examination included a natural science paper in which students were asked to write on the life of the fox, the otter and the hare. Countryman Kyffin was in his element but his father was puzzled by his success since his younger son had been getting consistently poor reports. One from Sopwith, the senior English master, was the cruellest. 'This boy has no power of lucid thought,' he wrote. Banks, the mathematics master, was equally scathing: 'Never have I met a boy with less ability.' His housemaster Cuthbert Mitford, a member of the notorious family which produced a series of fascist oddities, was particularly scornful. Kyffin remembered him as an incorrigible idiot who had never grown up and who did nothing but mock and laugh at him. He reported of Kyffin: 'He is the despair of all who teach him.'

When he saw the results of the school certificate, Harry Williams demanded an explanation. The headmaster, a Major Hardy, the father of actor Robert Hardy, replied that he had total confidence in his staff. Harry Williams wrote: 'If you have faith in your staff I have no confidence in the school and I intend to remove him.'

The result was that Kyffin was moved to yet another form which consisted of boys who were not going on to do a higher certificate. Among them was Richard Hillary, who was to become a Spitfire pilot and was badly burned and disfigured when his plane crashed. He wrote *The Last Enemy*, one of the finest accounts to emerge from World War Two.

Kyffin remembered him as a silent, sullen boy. At roll call he stood apart as though he felt himself too good to mix with lesser boys. He was a superb athlete, a very good oarsman, but would not train.

The form was given to a new master, a timid little man called McEachran who, it seemed, would be cannon fodder for the young toughs in the form. In the event his passion for poetry was such that it raised a spark in their minds. Kyffin believed it was McEachran's inspired teaching that awoke the talent in Hillary that later caused him to write. Indeed he felt a debt to McEachran for his own books, *Across the Straits* and *A Wider Sky*. To McEachran, poems were 'spells' and he later published an *Anthology of Spells*. He became a legend at the school.

Another pupil was 'Loopy' Ball. He came from Dublin and was a classmate of Richard Cobb who was to become professor of modern French history at Oxford and who researched his subject in France while living on the streets. They were both outsiders who did odd things.

The school chaplain was forever taking small boys out in his car. Richard Cobb rang him up and said, 'I am the Bishop of Bulawayo. I have been informed you are behaving in a very wrong way with small boys.' 'Frightened the life out of him and he behaved better after that,' commented Kyffin.

Though descended from a cloud of clerics, Kyffin was a lifetime unbeliever. A Shrewsbury chaplain may have contributed to this. He told the boys: 'Human beings are like unto peaches. They are smooth and beautiful on the outside but deep in the centre there is a nasty, gnarled stone. And this is sex.'

Cobb and Ball hatched a plan to murder Ball's hated mother by getting her into a Baby Austin and pushing her over a cliff near his home in southern Ireland. So far as Cobb was concerned, this was just juvenile fantasising. But the term after he had gone up to Oxford, a fellow undergraduate thrust a paper under his nose which told of the terrible murder of Mrs Ball in Dublin. Loopy had taken an axe to his mother and put her in the back of a Baby Austin, as he had planned. Unfortunately, with mummy in the back wrapped in a sack, it ran out of petrol in O'Connell Street. A passer-by helped Ball push the car to a petrol station where he filled up and drove for the cliff. Unhappily, the approach to the headland was a narrow lane which was blocked by a car with a courting couple inside. Ball had to stay there all night until the couple left and he was able to carry out his plan. He was quickly apprehended but when he appeared in court a Garda inspector called O'Reilly, who knew the family, spoke in his defence. He said: 'It was a very understandable thing for the young gentleman to do. She was a real old baggage.' Ball was given three years and then emigrated to Australia.

For Kyffin, the best parts of his time at Shrewsbury were visits to his relations, the Ramsays. Betty Mewies was another regular visitor. She recalled: 'My grandfather's sister Aunt Louisa married Andrew Ramsay, who had been Darwin's geologist on *The Beagle* and director of the Royal

Ordnance Survey. They met when Ramsay was on Anglesey researching for his book, which was the first to date the pre-Cambrian rock strata there. They had four daughters, Fanny, Ella, Violet and Dora. All tremendously eccentric old ladies. But very formal. During the war it didn't matter if you were only having spam for supper, you had to dress. As a girl of sixteen I thought it was marvellous to put on a long frock and be complimented by the housekeeper and the maids.

'Violet always carried a shopping basket with her. It contained her will and her best jewellery. She had two pairs of glasses, one for eating in. She would eat very, very quickly, then take them off and put the other pair on to talk. Dora's little fault was not her glasses but her teeth. Her top set didn't fit. She would very cleverly whip her handkerchief from her pocket and remove the teeth behind its cover. I remember once the teeth fell onto the carpet but everyone pretended they were not there. Dora thought that no one had ever noticed when she took out her teeth so cleverly and it would have been bad manners to disabuse her.

'The other three died but poor old Violet went on living for quite a time. She had a housekeeper called Maggie who was a wicked person who had Violet under her thumb. When Violet died Maggie inherited their lovely house and its contents.'

Artistic tuition was basic at Shrewsbury, though Kyffin retains a great affection for his art master, Woodruffe. In the art room was a drawer filled with prints. Art lessons consisted of choosing a print and copying it. Kyffin's parents asked Woodruffe to give him private lessons. It paid off. In his last summer term a prize was offered,

'Hardy's Painting Prize', for work done in the holidays. To Kyffin's astonishment, he won the prize. He was convinced the reason was the headmaster's wife was a relation.

For his prize he was asked to choose a book on art. 'Don't want a book on art,' he said. 'I want a book on hunting.' As Ernest Naish later recalled, Kyffin won over the objection of his headmaster.

There were unlooked for consequences of the win. Later in life when he was at loggerheads with Rollo Charles, the Keeper of Art at the National Museum of Wales, Charles told him he had also gone in for the prize that Kyffin won. Kyffin believed this rivalry was behind the huge differences of opinion he and Charles had over the respective merits of artists.

Despite his prowess, Kyffin had no thought to become an artist. His dream was to join the cavalry. Alas, there was no money left in the family coffers. His grandfather had sold all their land. That meant that Kyffin also had to abandon his second choice, which was to farm. In consolation, his father articled him to Yale and Hardcastle, a firm of land agents in Pwllheli. Captain Jack was scornful. 'You'll be in an office all day, sticking on stamps.'

The first day was rent day and that is exactly what Kyffin did. At the time he was living with his parents in Abererch. Although he vehemently claimed he had only a desultory interest in art, nevertheless every lunchtime he ran two miles home to paint a quick watercolour and then, lunchtime over, ran another two miles back to the office.

On Sundays he would leave the house at 2pm and run to the top of one of the peaks of Yr Eifl (the Rivals) and back in time to get to the house for the 6pm news.

It was here he began to paint portraits. One was of a

neighbour's little daughter, Jane, of T'yn Sarn, Abererch. To put her at her ease, Kyffin asked how she had spent the morning. 'Oh, we was all go to Pwllheli to buy presents,' she told him. 'Tom got a cap, Gwilym got a coat, I got two pairs of knickers.' 'What did brother Hughie get?' inquired Kyffin. 'Oh, Hughie is going to hospital in Bangor. So Hughie got a Holy Bible.'

There was little faith in hospital but much in heaven.

Chapter four

In their office in a passage between High Street and Penlan Street the partners Yale and Hardcastle were an unlikely pairing. George Frederick Cunningham Yale was an aristocrat. Impeccably dressed, he drove round the clients' land as though it were his. Donald Hardcastle on the other hand was English working class. Kyffin's was not the most arduous of jobs. He was allowed one day off a week for hunting and one day off for shooting over the company's estates.

Among Kyffin's duties was rudimentary architecture. He designed shippons for tenant farmers all over Llyn and restored the medieval hall on the 30,000-acre Nanhoron estate.

The Nanhoron and Broomhall estates were the biggest clients of the firm. The Broomhall estate was founded in the 19th century by a farmer, Rowland Jones. It is said that at his funeral there were two carriages. The first contained family mourners; the second contestants of the will. He had a grandson called Evans who qualified as a solicitor and took a job in London.

One day a woman came in seeking a divorce. The firm's principal refused to see her. Evans recognised the woman as one of William IV's illegitimate daughters who owned part of Regent Street, Greek Street and part of Golden Square. He offered to win the divorce case for her on condition she would marry him. He was a personable young man and the heiress agreed. In consequence, Broomhall became a rich estate of 30,000 acres. Their son,

Colonel Lloyd Evans, could walk from Pwllheli to Caernarfon on his own land.

The elder son, Rollie, was wildly eccentric. He hated the local rector so much he built a platform on the estate wall. Whenever the rector passed, Rollie climbed on the platform and bellowed at him like a bull. Another son, John, married an American girl Camille Clifford, described by those who knew her as having the beauty of the famous Gibson girls.

Kyffin worked for William, the younger son, when he inherited Broomhall. He was in the navy and went round the world with the Prince of Wales on *Renown*. Kyffin remembered that William hated the colour red. He was a keen pilot and would fly over his estate looking for tenants who had used red ridge tiles. If he found any he would land, climb into his Ford V8, drive into Pwllheli and storm into the office ordering the agents to get rid of the tiles.

One day, taxiing for take-off, he was blown off course into a bank of soil and killed. The estate was sold to Billy Butlin, who built a naval air station, *HMS Glendower*, at Pwllheli. After the war he recovered it and opened his first holiday camp there. Butlin tried to ingratiate himself with the locals. He booked the Old Vic company to put on a show in the big house. He invited all the people in Llyn and sent buses round the villages to pick them up. The excited audience filed into the hall and the performance began. They watched Laurence Olivier in total silence. At the end of the evening they all crept away to their buses, clearly disappointed. They had believed they were going to see Vic Oliver.

At the gateway to Llyn stands Glynllifon, a huge estate and the most magnificent neo-classical house in Wales. It was built by the first Lord Newborough, who believed his wife was the rightful queen of France.

Kyffin loved to tell the story of the last of the family to live in Glynllifon, the Hon Fred Wynn. 'He had plenty of money, lived as he liked and did not give a damn who he offended. He had two nephews. One was Tom (Lord Newborough), a bluff sort of mariner, and the other Colonel Vaughan Wynn, a cavalry officer who had fought in the South African war. Fred knew they hated each other. He would tell Lord Newborough he was going to inherit. The next week he would tell Vaughan and his wife Ruby the same thing. When he knew he was dying he sent for Vaughan and told him: "You are going to inherit so you might as well get ready. Bring along all your stock to the parkland here." Vaughan danced away with joy and had all his cattle and sheep sent to Glynllifon. Then the dreadful Fred Wynn breathed his last and when his will was proved it read: "I leave all my land at Glynllifon and all the stock upon it to my nephew Lord Newborough."

'Vaughan had to be content with becoming Tom Newborough's heir. Tom married three times in a campaign to get an heir so that Vaughan would not inherit. One of his wives, Denise, was a Hungarian Jewess, madam of a bawdy house in Shepherd Market, Mayfair. All to no avail. The dreaded Vaughan inherited.

'During his time Tom Newborough had cost the estate a fortune. He was showing the house to Sir Thomas Merton, a Jewish banker and great lover of the arts. On a dark wall outside the butler's pantry Sir Thomas saw a painting. He said: "Tom, I will give you five hundred pounds for that picture." Newborough told him not to be a damn fool but he agreed and Merton took away a Botticelli. It is a portrait of a young man holding a medallion and was used on a poster for a Royal Academy show of Italian treasures. Its value then was well over a million pounds.'

Kyffin's best friend at the time was Sandy Livingstone-Learmouth, a Hampshire Scot who had married the daughter of a slate mine owner in Blaenau Ffestiniog. They met shortly after Kyffin left Shrewsbury. Sandy suggested that Kyffin, now 18, should join the 6th Battalion the Royal Welch Fusiliers TA. Principally because, Sandy said, if he did he would get some good shooting.

There was no question of working his way through the ranks or facing a selection board. Sandy's word and Kyffin's background were enough to get him commissioned second lieutenant and appointed second in command of the Pwllheli platoon, which Sandy commanded.

Shortly after Kyffin joined, Hitler seized the opportunity to invade Poland and suddenly there were shooting opportunities all over Europe.

The Pwllheli platoon, it must be said, was not an excessively military formation. Kyffin recalled: 'I should not have passed the medical because I had already suffered my first epileptic attack. Luckily the MO was drunk. He stood swaying in the doorway, launched himself at me and gave me a terrible punch in the stomach. I went flat on the floor. He stood over me and said: Did you feel that? I said, no. Right, he said, give me your papers. He went into his office, I heard a clink of glass and when he came out he told me I had passed my medical.

'Our men were farm labourers and slaughterhouse attendants. One of them was Willy Christmas Jones, W C Jones. There was always a terrible row when the others

71

called him Shit-house Jones. We had another little man we called General Franco because he was the Spanish leader's double.

'The augurs of war were not good. We had a sergeant instructor called Nichol, of the Welsh Guards. When war broke out he shot himself in the armoury.

'On Sunday 3rd September I had to take church parade in Porthmadog. Archdeacon Jenkins told us from the pulpit: Doubtless in a few months' time you will all be blown to pieces. All the soldiers behind me went: Jesus.

'When we left Pwllheli to join the company at Porthmadog the word had gone round we were going to India. All the mothers and sisters and wives and girlfriends had turned up to wave us off, howling, We'll never see them again. When we left Porthmadog the mothers and sisters and wives and girlfriends came from Pwllheli and Beddgelert and Blaenau Ffestiniog and the word was: They are going to Egypt: we will never see them again. We went to Old Colwyn.

'At Old Colwyn I had to report our arrival to the Company Commander. I came to attention and slid under his desk, suffering from epilepsy...'

The amiable Colonel Davies remembered Kyffin and his friend Sandy coming to Hightown Barracks in Wrexham, the depot of the Royal Welch that had become an infantry training unit. There Kyffin got the shooting Sandy had promised him, though in a rather unorthodox way. Colonel Davies explained: 'Sandy was a very eccentric person. He introduced a bow and arrow into the Mess. He was very good with it. He always carried a pistol wherever he went. If he saw something in a field he wanted to take a pot shot at, he would stop the car, take out his pistol and shoot it.

'He and John (Kyffin) together made up a series of Crawshay Bailey songs. Some of these were published in a book with his (Kyffin's) cartoons but not the ones they sang in the regiment. I also remember the cartoons he did of his brother officers. They were brilliant and the regiment still treasures many of them.'

After training in Wrexham, Kyffin's battalion was ordered to Northern Ireland. He recalled: 'Our Company Sergeant Major Gwilym Jones, who looked like a Welsh forward, was the landlord of the Red Lion in Porthmadog. When he arrived at the station to embark he was as drunk as a lord. Major Edward Cadogan, our adjutant, was walking up and down when Gwilym came up the steps, dragging his rifle by the spout, with the butt banging on the steps. Cadogan started to remonstrate. Gwilym said: Look here, when we get to Ireland I'll bloody get you. Cadogan was so amazed he was speechless. In Ireland, before Cadogan had time to put him on a charge, Gwilym was sent on compassionate leave. The boat was torpedoed and he arrived back a hero.'

He told Kyffin: 'There was I in my underpants, shaving, and a bloody torpedo came right through the ablutions. I came out of the ship riding it like a jockey.' The ship sank, Gwilym survived and the charge was allowed to lie on the table.

Kyffin, Gwilym and the rest were part of the assembling 53rd Welsh Division. 'It was to have included a friend of mine, Philip Stable, the son of a High Court judge Sir Wintringham Stable,' said Kyffin. 'But he had to be moved quickly when his father sentenced some IRA men to death in Liverpool.

'One day some years later Sir Wintringham was caught speeding in Bala. After he had made a speech in mitigation, the presiding magistrate said: Sir Wintringham, you may remember that last year you came to talk to us about the law. In the course of your talk you told us we must never be bamboozled by legal jargon. Well, we are not going to be. We find you guilty.

'Later, out shooting on a blank day, Sir Wintringham eventually saw a rabbit cowering in a sheep fold. He raised his gun and was heard to mutter: And not even a Welsh jury is going to get you off this time.'

Alas, Kyffin's epileptic attacks which had dogged his youth were becoming more frequent and, despite urgent representations to everyone he thought might help, Kyffin was invalided out of the army which he loved.

Wendy Davies recalled: 'He always wanted to be a soldier. It was a terrible disappointment when his health broke down and he was invalided out. He was always a weedy looking individual but tough. And he didn't have any fits when out hunting.'

At the end of his life he was still musing on the cause of the condition. He believed it could have been the abuse he suffered as a tiny child at the hands of one of the nurses his mother had employed to look after him. Or perhaps it came with the meningitis he had when he was fifteen, or when his tonsils were ripped out. Significant, too, was this memory from his prep school:

> In the summer there were canoes for hire on the sea below the school. You could either go out on your own or in a pack. One day I went out with Dick and I got into a panic. I was suddenly petrified at the idea of drowning. It

74

had never happened before. It might have had something to do with the epilepsy because epileptics do get unreasoning panics.

I have always had amazing energy. I used to run from the sea at Pwllheli to the top of the Rivals (Yr Eifl). My doctor said it was due to an in-body supply of LSD. I can paint an eight foot picture in a day, which is something no other artist can do. And I feel better at the end of the day. When I get these epileptic attacks – and I still do as sort of shocks – they make me feel awful but they make me paint. It stimulates the brain and I can paint. I haven't had a *grand mal* for years and years. I get *petit mal* but, if I didn't, I wouldn't paint. It's all tied up.

It's odd how epilepsy scares people to death. I would never hide the fact that I was epileptic, partly because people have felt terribly guilty about being epileptic, especially women, and I wanted to break this. You don't hide the fact that you have arthritis. Even at Highgate School when I was teaching there I heard a couple of masters talking about a boy. One said: 'Of course you know he is epileptic and all epileptics are barmy.'

That attitude does an immense deal of harm. People go through life terrified because they are epileptic. If I talk about it I know other people will feel better for it.

In an odd way Kyffin was grateful for his disease. He told me: 'I have a feeling it is the clue to all my paintings. I have been compared to Van Gogh, who was also epileptic. It's true we came from the same social background; we both had highly strung mothers, and fathers who were well balanced; and we both had brothers who were worshipped by their mothers.'

Kyffin's first epileptic fit came in 1937 after spending a very cold day out shooting, followed by a regimental function at which he had one glass of port. He recalled: 'I went to bed and the next morning I was found under an open window with snow on me. I must have been struck as I got up to close the window. I had a second attack a few hours later. Sandy drove me home barely conscious. My doctor sent me to Lord Cohen, a very distinguished surgeon with a practice in Rodney Street, Liverpool. He gave me a lumbar puncture and made a mess of it. He hit the vertebrae and it was unbelievably painful. I was in such pain that when we got to Port Dinorwic, on the way to Caernarfon, I had to be taken out and laid on the floor of the Halfway House (a pub).

'The next attack came the morning after a dance at the Goat in Beddgelert. On that occasion I had nothing to drink but the next day when I went for my lunch of beans on toast I had an attack in the street.'

What is certain is the value of the work that Kyffin did throughout his life to help others suffering from the disease.

Miriam Rees of Conwy worked among epileptics as a social worker. She said: 'The epilepsy has meant that Kyffin has missed so much in life because of his illness. But by publicly admitting he suffers from epilepsy he has done a massive amount to help others. Most epileptics hide their disease but Kyffin is never afraid to put his head over the parapet. It takes a lot of doing because the disease frightens other people.'

Eileen Evans of Llanrwst ran a support group for epileptics in Bangor. 'My son was an epileptic,' she told me. 'He hanged himself when he was thirty. He found he had got nowhere in life. Epilepsy affected his social life, his career, his education, everything. I found him hanging from a banister at his home in Bethesda. My son was intelligent enough to know he was going nowhere in life and was better out of it. Who knows? Perhaps he was right.

'Sufferers desperately want to be treated as normal people. They hate people to hover over them. The problem is that when a carer knows it is possible for them to lose balance in some of the most dangerous situations – in my son's case mountain climbing – it can turn the carer into a nervous wreck. Even walking by a river can be dangerous.

'Epilepsy has a devastating effect. I speak from experience. People don't understand it. Someone crashes down, writhing and kicking. It's natural for the people round them to be afraid. People are fine with epileptics until they see them in a fit. From then on they are cagey about being around.'

When Kyffin agreed to become involved with Mrs Evans' epilepsy support group at Ysbyty Gwynedd (Gwynedd Hospital), Bangor, she was delighted. She said:

> We immediately struck up a rapport. I said, 'I believe you would be willing to become president.' He said, 'Good God, no. I don't want to be a figurehead: I will be chairman.'
>
> It was as much down to the fact that we had such a charismatic chairman as my hard graft that we got the association off the ground. He arranged sensational Christmas parties at Plas Mawr in Conwy, Penrhyn Castle and Cochwillan, a medieval house near Bangor that was once the home of Archbishop Williams, an erudite cleric who fought on both sides in the Civil War. Over the fourteen years I ran it, I hope we managed to bring the illness out of the darkness and get people to realise that epileptics are no different from other people.

I frankly doubt that epilepsy gives you talent but it is true that Van Gogh, Edward Lear and Julius Caesar were epileptics. I am always loath to attribute anything to such an illness. But the similarities between Kyffin and Van Gogh are definitely there. I have a very large folder containing his letters and cards. On the outside I have written to the children: Take very great care of the contents. I have no doubt that one day Kyffin will be as famous as Van Gogh.

To have been recognised to the extent he was in his lifetime is remarkable. I remember an *Antiques Roadshow* expert on TV valued one of his paintings at £15,000. Kyffin always wondered why people bought his paintings. He didn't want his paintings to be more than ordinary people could afford.

For sufferers, epilepsy is an absolutely dreadful burden. Kyffin started off life without epilepsy. He thought he had some peculiar episode when he was about seven and then nothing again for years. This often happens. In his case, it affected his career for the best. He is one of the few people who could say illness had given them something. When he first told me he had got diabetes as well, I was devastated because I had been making him birthday cakes. I thought, my God, I could have killed him. There he was with undisclosed diabetes and I was feeding him great chunks of rich fruit cake. He could have gone into a coma and I would have been responsible for killing off Wales's most famous artist.

What I find tragic about Kyffin is that he has a great deal of love to give to a person. It was blown up in his face because of his ill health. It got between him and his girl. He was so understanding and kind and generous to the group. Epileptics are obsessive and it may account for the frenzied rate at which he painted. When they find something they like doing, they use it as an escape. It is a sinister illness. Kyffin hunted in the mountains. That takes a lot of bravery. It is easier to live a sheltered life.

I remember him telling me once he had gone to Cwm Bychan to paint and he honestly felt the mountains were coming down on him. To stay there and continue to paint takes tremendous courage.

Lady Crickhowell, the wife of the former Secretary of State for Wales Nicholas Edwards and a friend to Kyffin of many years' standing, also suffered from mild epilepsy as a result of an operation that went wrong. She told me: 'I take the same drug as Kyffin. Once you find the level of the dosage it is all right and you can live a normal life, even get a driving licence, as Kyffin and I both did.'

Eluned Ann Thomas, a member of the Welsh Language Society, took over the support group from Kyffin. She said at her home in Bodedern: 'Kyffin used his influence to get us a room at the hospital to meet in. His influence is always available when an epileptic needs help. He is a kind and good man. Very gentle. I was surprised that he was so keen on the army. He is so gentle he comes over as a pacifist. I do think his mother did him a great deal of harm when she prevented him from speaking Welsh. He is *Cymry Cymraeg*. Had he been allowed to speak Welsh he would have been another Cynan, our greatest bard. He knows a lot more Welsh than he lets on but I think he is too shy to use it. You can tell his love for the language by the loving way he pronounces the words.

'He wants people to speak in their mother tongue. Deep down he misses it because he feels so Welsh. As a painter he speaks to people who are not interested in art. The young farmers round here go mad for one of his animal postcards or a farm print. He understands ordinary people so well.'

Mrs Thomas met Kyffin through the support group. She explained: 'My husband John is an epileptic. We went in and Kyffin was the chairperson. We were unaware of his importance. He is our greatest ambassador because he has never tried to hide his epilepsy. The only time I have seen him angry was when Reginald Bosanquet, the TV news reader, accidentally disclosed he was an epileptic. Kyffin was furious that he hadn't already disclosed it to help combat the fear people have of the disease. There is still prejudice. For instance, there was a boy we were helping who had a fit on the bus from Bangor to his home in Caernarfon. They just threw him off because they thought it was drugs. We get examples of people being barred from shops because they have had *grand mals*. My husband John's mother never told anyone he had epilepsy and my father was very upset that I was marrying a sufferer. Imagine what it must have been like when Kyffin was young.

'He was very affected by Eileen's son's suicide. I can remember him saying to me: I understand his depression. And I thought: You probably suffer in the same way. I think it is the epilepsy that gives Kyffin his energy.

'It doesn't matter who you are or what you are he welcomes you to his friendship.'

Chapter five

Kyffin returned to civilian life completely defeated and in his own eyes far from a hero. He had fought a series of impressive battles with medical boards but their verdicts had been unanimous. He had no future as a soldier.

It was a crushing blow. Since boyhood, Kyffin had wanted to be a professional soldier. Ideally in the cavalry. He saw himself leading his men in a do or die charge. Now he realised the nearest he was going to get to war was the Home Guard. He could not even go back to his job as a land agent. The army doctors had told him the examinations would tax him too severely. He did not take seriously their suggestion he should become a painter. That was not a job: it was a hobby.

There was one consolation. When he returned to his home on the Llyn it was to find that his mother had taken on a land girl. A very beautiful land girl who moved like a gazelle. Her name was Gwyneth Griffith. The Williamses had no land but Gwyneth, who was between jobs, had agreed to help with the housework while she was looking for a place on a farm. Although he did not realise it at the time, it was probably the most important meeting of Kyffin's life. Gwyneth was a brilliant artist and the best student of her year at the Slade School of Art. For the moment, though, it was enough that she was beautiful and moved like a gazelle. Not for the first time, Kyffin fell in love. Unfortunately Mrs Williams noticed – and disapproved.

Kyffin recalled: 'Gwyneth's time with us was fated.

There were terrible rows. She was sent packing and went to work at a farm at Llandegai, a big Penrhyn Estate farm at the bottom of the Nantfrancon pass, where she fell deeply in love with a farm boy who seemed to dominate her. Some years later a doctor in Swansea read *Across the Straits* in which I wrote about her. He wrote to tell me his father had a farm near Bangor and he knew Gwyneth. He came to see me and kept saying what a lovely girl she was. I realised he was the farm boy. He never married her.

'Gwyneth was a very sensitive, delicately-featured girl. Her father came from St David's and her mother was a Lewis of Montgomeryshire. She was very dreamy and used to wander round in a state of permanent drowsiness. I found her extremely good company but she would have nothing to do with me. She was a lovely, gentle girl.'

The lovely, gentle girl hooted with laughter when Kyffin's words were recounted to her in the ground floor flat near Trefor Bridge, in Llangollen, where she lived after retiring from her job as art mistress at a girls' school in the town.

'He wouldn't think that if he could see me now at 83,' she said. 'I was very cross with him when he wrote in *Across the Straits* about me moving like a gazelle. I was teaching at the time and they gave me a terrible time in the common room.

'It is true I had been at the Slade and I got on well there. But I was too lazy to be an artist. I won a prize but I have never had any respect for my work. I never hang my own paintings in the flat. To be honest, the idea of being shut up in a studio repelled me. My grandmother was a farmer's wife and I wanted to farm. As a young girl I said if I couldn't farm I wanted a job with animals. Painting came a very bad third, something John could never understand.

'We did lots of things together but I never realised he was sweet on me. In fact, I don't think he really understood women. I know he was very disappointed that I was not as interested in painting as he was. I had pretty well given it up. I took my paints and easel round the farms where I worked but I did not even unpack them. I remember once he took me sketching to Nantperis. He had his sketchbook and a bottle of ink and was soon drawing away. I didn't even take mine out. I just stood there shivering, wishing he would take me for a cup of tea. I was certainly not a compulsive painter in the way that he was. But I always enjoyed his company. He was great fun.

'He loved shooting rabbits and insisted on teaching me to shoot. We began with clay pigeons and when he thought I was ready he took me out with a gun looking for a sitting target. We found one at last but I was very reluctant and by the time I had brought the gun up I was glad to see the sitting target had run off. He was not pleased.'

It was Gwyneth who launched him on his career. 'I saw some watercolours he had painted. I was very impressed and I advised him to contact the Slade. In fact I wrote to the head of the school, Professor Randolph Schwabe, recommending him. Mrs Williams was a very possessive woman and it was a long time before she forgave me for getting him into the Slade and taking him away from home. I believe she did him a great deal of harm. I remember once we were sitting by the Menai Strait and he said: I can never marry: I am epileptic. I had never heard that epilepsy was a bar to marriage but his mother had told him he must never marry. His father wouldn't have said anything. I am afraid he just did as he was told.

'When he was at the Slade, John wrote to say he was worried about his mother living alone after her husband died. He asked me to move in with her but I refused. It would not have done.'

She looked wistful when she said: 'All I have to remind me of him is a sketch he gave me. I went to his studio determined to buy one. On the wall was this lovely rock-scape with waves crashing against them and over all a setting sun. I asked how much it was and he said £500, which was beyond my pocket. I looked through some sketches and came across one that was obviously a preliminary sketch for the rock-scape. He gave it to me and it has been on my wall ever since.

'I know he thought the Arts Council was against him but when I was teaching I met an Arts Council official who thought he was a fine man and a great painter. But he said rather wistfully: I do wish he wouldn't teach people to paint like he does. I knew what he meant. Kyffin looks easy to imitate but his imitators cannot put that extra piece of magic into the picture that Kyffin can.'

Kyffin was astonished at the notion of going to art school. He had no wish to be an artist. If he could not be a soldier, or a land agent, he would settle for a job as a schoolmaster. He went to Gabbitas and Thring to try to get a job in a prep school and while he was waiting for an appointment took a job with Windsor and Newton as a salesman. No teaching job materialised.

When he was offered an interview for the Slade he was amazed. The letter asked for examples of his work. He had none, so he copied a Paul Nash painting of widgeon winging over marshes from a cigarette card and sent that. Amazingly, he received a letter giving him an interview with the school, which at that time had been evacuated to Oxford. Afterwards he always explained his acceptance by saying it was wartime and the Slade had very few male students.

Kyffin recalled: 'I stayed in a pub in Oxford and went for my interview the next day. Schwabe was a very well mannered man but he looked horrified when I showed him my sketchbooks. However, he offered me a place, and in a sort of dream, I accepted it.'

At Oxford, the Slade was merged with the Ruskin School of Art and had two professors, Schwabe and Albert Rutherston, who had been Ruskin master of drawing. It was housed in a wing of the Ashmolean Museum and the ratio of girls to men was eight to one. Kyffin joined the school in October 1941. He lodged in Observatory Street with the Singletons, a glorious, if feckless, Irish family with a son who played the saxophone incessantly. He was a little odd, Kyffin was told, in consequence of a Dublin coal man emptying a sack of coals on his head.

From the first day, Kyffin believed Schwabe had made a mistake. 'It was terrifying because all these girl students could draw like angels and lots of them looked like angels too,' Kyffin told me. 'I had never really drawn at all and I just could not do it. We had a thing called the Sketch Club. Students were encouraged to do their own work and send it in to be judged. The tutor in charge of the Sketch Club was a man called Barnet Freedman. He was a bully. He was terribly rude to the girls. He would go up to an easel and say: I suppose the colour is all right and the drawing and the composition. Do you know what I think you ought to do with it? Then he would pause and add: Put it under the sink and stand on it.

'With me, he was even ruder. I went up to Boar's Hill outside Oxford and did three watercolours. I put them on the dais with the work of the other students. When Freedman came along to criticise he said: When I first saw these I said, Great Scott! When I looked for a second time I said, Good Lord! When I saw them a third time I said, Heaven help him! I stayed away from the Club for a week after that.

'Fortunately, Alan Gwyn Jones also taught at the Slade. He was a wonderful artist and I learnt a lot from him. He was a descendant of John Jones of Maesygarnedd (a co-signatory of the death warrant of Charles I), and won the DSO with the Welsh Guards. He was one of the finest portrait painters in Britain but could never get an exhibition in Wales. The Arts Council said they had never heard of him. Then, at the end of his life, just as he was going blind, the Tate gave him a retrospective. That woke the Arts Council. They gave him one too. At the Swansea Eisteddfod he won the gold medal and a week later he died.'

Kyffin insisted drawing did not come easily to him. 'I had to learn. All the others were good before they went there. They went there because they had talent. I went there for the good of my health and I couldn't draw. I did win a couple of portrait prizes but I can't think how. Or why I was awarded the Robert Ross leaving scholarship of £10. I think it was sheer nepotism. I got on very well with Schwabe because I shared my lodgings in Observatory Street with his sister-in-law. One day I was walking along the High with him and he stopped and said: Oh Williams, I have got a scholarship and I always forget to give it. Would you like it? I said: Thank you very much...'

Tom Griffiths, who was at the Slade with Kyffin, recalled at his London flat that he was a loner.

> Coming from the army he was older than most of us at Slade. He did not join a group, let alone a gang, so we weren't really aware of him. He has said he drifted through Slade. Of course he did much more. Like all artists, he took what nourishment he needed. He took as much of Slade drawing as he needed and did not become a slave to pretty line as most of us did.
>
> William Coles, whom John wrote about as 'Maurice Wood' in his book *A Wider Sky*, was a bit older than the average student and they became good friends. Coles once made a perceptive and appreciative remark to me about John's work. He thought he had much natural facility and, where others might have come to rely on superficial effects, he deliberately made challenges for himself. One of which was using the palette knife which was a most un-Slade approach.
>
> William Coles had a deep feeling for tonal values, another un-Slade virtue, and I think John was usefully influenced by this whilst always remaining true to himself. If he appeared to drift, it was because most of his fellow students could not have appreciated his stick-ability – more important in the long run than fashionable cleverness. Actually he was by no means a tortoise, as the rapidity of his cartoons and his decisive mastery of character in portraiture show. He was much cleverer, both as an artist and a man, than we other students appreciated in our self-absorption. Both Randolph Schwabe and Albert Rutherston liked him and became good friends. They were not fools.

Kyffin thought he knew why he was improving. 'I was lucky because, unlike the rest of the students at the Slade, I knew exactly what I wanted to paint: the land where my family had lived for a thousand years. Other people who were far better artists were floundering around trying to get the effects of light, which was quite beside the point. I never worried because I knew I hadn't any talent. To begin with, everything was very frustrating but I wasn't all that bothered by early failure.'

To Kyffin the student, art was a skill, reproducing on paper something you see before you. All that changed one day in the Ashmolean Library when he took down a book on Piero della Francesca.

'I turned over the pages mechanically until I came to a sudden stop. There was Piero's *Resurrection*, with the sublime figure of Christ rising from the tomb above the sleeping soldiers. My initial reaction was shock, followed by a feeling of intense emotion. I gazed at this beautiful picture until I could no longer see it for my tears which were rolling down my cheeks.

'It was the amazing compassion which Piero had managed to put into the eyes of Christ. Here was a face of such strength and love that for the first time I began to realise what great art is. An intangible thing, impossible to rationalise, and far removed from mere representation.'

In that moment Kyffin, the artist, was born.

'It totally changed my artistic life. I realised there was something more to painting. There was a spiritual element which is indefinable. A power to move. It wasn't the religious aspect: it was the beauty of the painting. Because of that, I stumbled on, trying desperately now to become a painter. I was heartened when I learnt that St Paul was an epileptic too. His conversion on the road to Damascus has all the aspects of an epileptic fit with lights and visions.'

Rosalie Williams, the daughter of wealthy parents, arrived at the Slade a year after Kyffin. At her home in Lewes, Sussex, she recalled that after her strict upbringing by a governess, the Slade was a cultural shock.

'I disapproved of girls going into men's rooms; indeed a lot of the behaviour was very strange to me. There was also a certain amount of hostility because I came from a wealthy background, though I certainly didn't flaunt it. My best friend, Yvonne Hudson, came from a poor background. We lived together on the college barge and did fire-watching duties for one shilling and sixpence an hour.

'Kyffin once told me he remembered a dress I wore at the Slade Ball. I am not surprised. I wore the same dress every year. He wasn't like the other students. He was never arrogant and didn't look down on us because we were girls.

'I am very slow to make friends and he kept his emotions to himself. But I liked his attitude as a student. We didn't have what is nowadays called a relationship but we were very close. He was serious and he worked hard. It was obvious that he had a great talent. He had to work at his drawing, I know, but some people have facile talent. They explode like a firework and you think they are going to do great things but they just disappear. Kyffin developed slowly and greatly. I go to all his exhibitions and I am happy to say we are still in touch.'

After she left the Slade, Rosalie married a well-known actor in his day, Hugh Sinclair. 'We saw a lot of Kyffin and Hugh liked him as much as I did.'

Sadly, Hugh died suddenly. Rosalie remembers Kyffin was a tower of strength. 'He was always there when I needed him. I was very surprised when one day he suddenly proposed marriage. Fond though I was of him, it would have been impossible. I'd a very close and happy marriage and Hugh had died suddenly. I had to accustom my children to the loss of their father. I felt I couldn't uproot them from everything they knew, with its associations with their father, and take them to live in Wales. Of course, it would have been quite unthinkable to take Kyffin out of Wales.'

Her son Nicholas, an art photographer to whom Kyffin was godfather, said that Kyffin would have made a wonderful father. 'He was always there for me, as he was for my mother. He painted my portrait when I was nine years old, he helped me in my career and all his life was a wonderful friend. He was incredibly warm when my father died. He used to phone and visit regularly. My mother always said he was the nicest person of all the students when she was at the Slade.'

To a deeply susceptible man like Kyffin, the Slade where men were in a minority was a honey trap.

'I was unofficially engaged to a lovely girl called Leila Troup but after a year at the Slade she went off to join the WRNS. She took me to her home in Hampshire. It was disastrous. Her father was a very nice man, chairman of the Hampshire War Agricultural Committee. Her mother was Russian, the least intelligent member of the Moscow intelligentsia. She was a snob and she had been told all Welshmen were common. Her husband, who had been wounded at Gallipoli, had developed epilepsy and she was determined her daughter would not marry a Welsh epileptic. She forced her to marry someone else. I don't think I ever got over it.

'The engagement was never official because her parents

would never allow it but what followed has always baffled me because, as students, we got on well and we were deeply in love. Yet she has never since, in all her life, had one word of praise for anything I have ever done. I do not know why this is. It wasn't that she didn't like me. She will never let go of me, but still, after all these years, she never ever says anything favourable about me. She comes to all my exhibitions and just laughs at my paintings. It is some strange inhibition. It still hurts.'

In 1998, Leila, at her home in Blockley, Gloucestershire, was puzzled by these observations. She insisted she had always known of his promise and dedication and she went on: 'It has been marvellous to watch his success and to see his health improve. We saw him for the last time last year when he called in on his way to Highgrove. Prince Charles had invited him to see his pictures. We wiped his car and generally tidied him up. He seemed to enjoy it very much.'

She recalled how they had met in the Ashmolean and spent romantic hours together fire-watching from the top of the building.

She confessed: 'I adored him but the war interfered with long-term plans and my mother disliked the idea of her future son-in-law being a poor art student. I was never taken to meet his parents but he used to come to my Hampshire home for weekends and I recall we spent a lot of time walking. I think, in his London days, he missed the sea and the open places.

'He did one curious picture at this time which consisted of three heavy lines of paint. Blue (sky), red (poppies), and green (fields), which did not impress us very much.'

At 80, Kyffin cheerfully admitted that he was still susceptible to a pretty face but insisted he was not attractive to women. In considerable opposition to the evidence, it should be added.

Nevertheless, he insisted: 'It's been a total mystery to me. I always thought I would be a good husband and father. The trouble is I can never show off. I did not court very well. Some men pretend they are nicer than they really are to impress the opposite sex. I felt they should accept me for what I was and they never did.'

More than anything, Kyffin wanted to marry, but his epilepsy always got in the way.

'That has been my tragedy,' he told me. 'My priority in life was always to get married. Painting was not then a priority. I have always loved women. It is strange that the two girls I very badly wanted to marry had fathers who were epileptic. There was Leila and then a German girl. The extraordinary thing about her was that I sensed the moment I met her that she was illegitimate. How, I do not know. Her father and mother lived in Geneva and he had been in the German army. The girl – even after all these years I do not want to name her – used to come over from Switzerland to see me. On one visit she told me she had just learnt that her mother was not her real mother. Apparently, during the war in an air raid on Berlin, a girl appeared at her family home with a bundle which she gave to her father. She said: 'This is your daughter!' and disappeared.

'When I knew her she was still racked with guilt about the German treatment of the Jews. Later, while she was studying in the medical school in Geneva, she met an American Jewish doctor and married him.'

Kyffin believed that in terms of romance his life had been

one of near misses. 'I have had lots of girlfriends but when it came to the crunch they all ran,' he said. 'When I was at the Slade, Jack Baer, who owned the Hazlitt Gallery, would come in to draw. He is now the most respected art dealer in London. His cousin Derek married Roger Williams-Ellis's cousin Elizabeth. I was terribly in love with her too, but at the time I was having epileptic attacks in quick succession.

'The truth is girls despised me in those days. I was unhealthy, I hadn't any money and I really had no talent at all. Talent comes out through obsession. You can never create obsession. But if you have obsession you can create talent. I had obsession and my obsession was to put down the mountains on canvas or paper. It still is. My art is made up of the people, the landscape and the sea. It started in my hunting days. I developed a sort of mental computer that stored images I could recall later. It's a very odd thing. You can train yourself to have a visual memory. It's like having a TV screen in your head that you can turn on at will. But that only comes with experience and continual thinking.

'Another odd thing is that I could create my own music in my head and hear the individual instruments playing. Very often I could do this on the Underground or on horseback. Movement would turn it on and I could listen for hours to my own music. I couldn't write it down because I do not know a note of music. I played the piano very badly but it was very gratifying to be able to listen to my own music.'

Unlucky in love, Kyffin was equally unlucky in war. He was desperate to test his courage in action and just once it seemed he had a chance.

'A very nice Australian Air Force man called Bill

Morrison came to draw in the Slade. He knew I felt guilty about being invalided out when my generation was fighting. One day he said: We are going out on exercise in the north of Scotland. We are going to bomb an island. Would you like to come? I said it sounded rather fun and he said: Put on your Home Guard uniform and come along to the airfield. I will get you in a Wellington. No one will know.

'He got his air crew to keep the officers occupied while he smuggled me into the bomb bay. The engine started turning. I waited for the take off. Suddenly I heard a bellowing. I had been spotted and I was hauled out. The next week he went on a raid and never came back.

'We students used to go to an aircraft dump on the Iffley road to examine the wrecks of Dorniers, Messerschmitts and Heinkels. I remember seeing Paul Nash out there, wrapped up in mufflers because he was terrified of catching cold. He was drawing them for his finest paintings, those of planes washed up on the shores of England.'

Desperate to play some part in a war his generation was fighting, Kyffin joined the North Company of Oxford Home Guard. The platoon he commanded was as eccentric a body of men as any army ever held since Falstaff's company of hirelings.

One of his soldiers, Haford Gregory, would never come to Sunday parades. Kyffin rooted him out in Jesus College and ordered him to parade the next Sunday. Gregory demurred. He said: 'That's more than my life's worth. My father runs the Lord's Day Observance Society in Wales.'

Kyffin, who knew the army, planned to test the Home Guard by mounting an invasion on Oxford the next

Sunday. He insisted on Gregory attending. 'It was soon obvious that Gregory was the most bloodthirsty soldier of them all,' he recalled. 'I saw him climb on the roof of a tank and hammer on the top with the butt of his rifle. Odd how the theology students were usually the fiercest soldiers.'

Kyffin's platoon sergeant Charles Parker was a dandy who wore a beautifully cut barathea uniform instead of the harsh serge army issue. He loved lecturing on the bren gun and dismantled the gun with loving care. But when Kyffin, by then president of the Slade Society, asked him to lecture to the students on old master drawings, upon which he was the greatest living authority, he refused. He said he never gave lectures. It was he, incidentally, who discovered the Tom Keating forgeries.

Corporal Atkinson was another platoon member. 'He was in charge of our armoury,' Kyffin recalled. 'He had been a captain in the South African war and a sergeant in the First World War. He was a distinguished military historian of Exeter College, very eccentric and subject to violent hatreds, one of which was women students. He would not tolerate them. When they came to his lectures he would address them as "Gentlemen". He sometimes took his trousers down in their presence and warmed his bottom at the fire.

'Another hatred was of Brasenose men. He had a series of black cocker spaniels called Jumbo. He would take them onto the wall of Brasenose and set them on the students. The dogs came to know all the Brasenose men and used to bite them in the street.

'My Uncle Jack Kyffin, who lived in Oxford, was also a member of the Home Guard. He had been a colonel in the RAMC in World War 1 and a great boxer, who won his last fight at the age of sixty. He claimed he won because his opponent was a corporal who could not bear to strike an officer, a court martial offence in other circumstances. In the Home Guard, although he was merely a medical orderly with the rank of private, it did not deter him from putting his commanding officer on a charge for being late.'

Kyffin's platoon was nothing if not enthusiastic. He recalled with a shudder the night they went too far: 'We were doing exercises and we came across a caravan that, unbeknown to us, a pair of lovers were using. One of my platoon threw a thunder flash under the caravan and out dashed a man in his underpants and a woman in her nightie.'

With such distractions, it was a wonder that Kyffin was able to make the progress he did with his art, yet somehow he managed to scrape through his first terms and was told he could stay for another year.

He was barely back in Oxford for the new term when his father died after an attack of bronchitis. Not for the first time his mother's behaviour baffled him. He wrote in *Across the Straits*:

> After the burial service she entertained the mourners as if she were presiding over a normal tea party. I felt sure that as soon as it was over she would crack, but she didn't. From that day on she never mentioned his name again and she seemed to want to forget him as she went back into the world of her father.

Another tragedy followed. Back at the Slade, Kyffin received a letter from the commanding officer of a battle school in the south of England. Two days earlier his beloved brother Dick had stepped on a bakelite percussion hand grenade and blown off his left foot. Kyffin recalled that on the same day his own left foot had unaccountably swelled up. He had been in agony for twelve hours until it just as suddenly subsided. Later his brother told him this apparently telepathic communication had occurred half an hour before his own accident.

Kyffin claimed that there was little tuition at the Slade in his day. He remembered Professor Borenius, a shy, gentle man and desperately uncommunicative. His voice in lectures on the history of art was so soothing that most of his students fell asleep. His examinations were a farce, Kyffin claimed. He would arrive in the lecture hall, immaculate in morning coat and bearing twelve lantern slides that he flashed onto a screen. Students were required to date the painting on the screen, ascribe it to a school and identify the painter. To ensure success, they formed groups and each member learnt a different period of art history, so that, as a painting flashed on the screen, the student who had studied that particular period could identify it to his friends. Not surprisingly, everyone took first class honours in that particular subject.

In the life classes there was always a shortage of models and it fell to Kyffin to tour Oxford, press-ganging and bribing strangers to pose. But there were also consolations. On one memorable day Lord Berners came in to draw next to him. He went to a lecture by Jan Mazaryk, the Czech Foreign Minister who later died in mysterious circumstances, and met refugees like Leonid Pasternak, Boris's father and a very good painter. He made a friend of the cartoonist H M Bateman, who sat at the next 'pig' –

easel – to Kyffin, drawing deeply serious life studies. He told Kyffin that the war had killed his sense of fun and he could no longer draw the caricatures for which he was internationally famous. Nevertheless, he drew a memorable one of Kyffin in which he looks like a dodgy car salesman or racing tout. Kyffin loved it.

Kyffin believed his own drawing was slow to progress. Professor Schwabe looked at one, sighed heavily and said, 'Oh Williams, why do you always make your nudes look like oak trees? You cannot draw, you had better see if you can paint.'

It was the beginning of the greatest love affair in Kyffin's life. Years later he wrote:

> I found the rich pigment appealed to my sensuous nature. As I tackled my first life painting I fell completely under the spell of paint and produced something which, even if it was incompetent, was unlike anything else in the school. The more I painted, the more I realised that this was my real means of expression. When my third year came to an end I won the Slade Portrait prize.

Chapter six

Kyffin left the Slade with two ambitions: to become an art teacher in a public school and to marry a delightful wife. As was to happen so often in his life, the hour produced the man. Though not, alas, the woman.

His Home Guard commander, Major Greswell, was secretary of the Oxford University Appointments Board. On Kyffin's behalf, he wrote glowing letters to every public school in the country. A considerable number expressed interest and Kyffin began a scholastic tour in order to sell himself.

Sadly, selling himself was never one of Kyffin's talents. Aiming high, the first school he tried was Harrow because the headmaster, R H Moore, had been an assistant master at Shrewsbury in Kyffin's day. In his office there was what Kyffin took to be a mat in front of the fire. Only when the mat got to its feet, staggered across the room and bit him did he realise it was an elderly cocker spaniel. Obviously sharing the dog's opinion, Moore turned his old pupil down.

Hearing that the assistant art master of Christ's Hospital was about to be sacked, he tried there. He was turned down. At his next attempt, Merchant Taylors, he was short-listed but in the end the job went to his rival who, it turned out, was the former assistant art master at Christ's Hospital.

He was successful at last when he went for an interview at Highgate School. The headmaster, Geoffrey Bell, was a genial man and took to Kyffin at once. He not only got the job: he was appointed to command the Signals Platoon of the school Officers' Training Corps. It proved to be a sinecure. The boys were infinitely more knowledgeable about radio than Kyffin. Wisely, he let the platoon run itself, which it did with considerable efficiency.

Delighted with his luck in at last getting a job as an art master, Kyffin went to the Royal Academy to look at pictures. There he met his former Slade tutor, the sadistic Barnet Freedman, to whom he broke the news. Freedman, characteristically discouraging, said: 'Well, that is you finished as an artist.'

'I have to teach, I have no money,' Kyffin explained. 'No artist worth his salt ever worried about money,' was the crushing reply.

Telling the story of this cruel snub many years later, the generous Kyffin had to add that, for all his faults, Freedman was a fine artist who did some marvellous illustrations for Siegfried Sassoon's *Memories of an Infantryman*.

Kyffin's salary for teaching six days a week was £300 a year. It would have gone up to £350 if he had taken a House. 'Couldn't do it,' he admitted. 'It was bad enough spending days with boys. To spend the nights as well would have been hell. I couldn't even bear to eat with them. I used to go into Highgate village to a little cafe.'

The boys had a better opinion of Kyffin than he had of them. They appreciated his belief that art and punishment were incompatible. A teacher who refused to punish was bound to be popular. The more anarchic of his pupils began to play on this belief. One day when he told the class how the National Gallery's art collection had been moved to Wales for safety, it erupted with laughter. With difficulty, Kyffin won silence and asked what was so funny. 'Oh sir,' said one boy, 'it wouldn't be very safe there.' 'Why not?' asked Kyffin. 'Well sir, you know the rhyme. Taffy was a Welshman, Taffy was a thief…'

The torment lasted only a year. By then, even the small boys he taught realised that Kyffin was something special and his lessons became among the most popular in the school. That remained true during the 27 years he taught there.

One boy asked if he was married and was told he wasn't. 'I thought not,' said the boy. 'You are always so cheerful.' Another said: 'Oh Mr Williams, I understand you are the greatest living artist.' 'Stuff and nonsense,' said Kyffin. 'Who on earth told you that?'… 'Sir, the postman in Taplow.'

When a boy behaved really badly he would ask his housemaster to flog him. He recalled: 'A boy called Winterbottom just would not stop talking. I asked his housemaster, John Coombes, to flog him. He said: I cannot beat Winterbottom: his father is going to get me two tickets for the Cup Final.

'I taught Warren Mitchell's son. A nice lad. Swings and roundabouts. Had another boy, Pickering, who was incorrigibly naughty. One night he shinned out down a rope and escaped from school. At the time, part of Hampstead Lane was being dug up and there were lights surrounding the hole. Pickering moved the lights and a car went into the hole. The Head arranged to have him moved to another school. I saw him later and he said: Oh sir, it's not a patch on Highgate. The discipline is appalling.

'When I was leaving a little boy came up and said: You cannot leave, you are the best master in the whole school. You never punish anybody. It was flattering to be liked but I was not a natural teacher. A boy would ask: Please sir, how do horses go, sir? I would tell him to take a pair of spectacles for his model and draw a couple of round things. How do cows go? Do a rectangle, I'd say. If a boy asked what he should draw, I would think of an animal I knew how to draw and pressurise, say, an elephant into a boy's mind.'

Some of his pupils had dazzling careers.

'Hoffnung left the term before I came but Geoffrey Palmer, the actor, was a pupil. I did the scenery for a school production of *Journey's End*. Palmer was in it with Christopher Moran, who directed *Jewel in the Crown* for TV.'

Two other pupils, Anthony Green and Patrick Proctor, are both Royal Academicians.

'I didn't teach Proctor anything. When he came to leave he took me out to tea to tell me what an awful art master I was. A few years later, he brought his portfolio and said he was anxious to become an artist. He went to the Slade and within three years he had his first one man show. His pictures filled every gallery in the Redfern and everything was sold before the exhibition opened. I did produce some good boys in my time but I thought the reason was less to do with me than that Highgate drew on a highly intelligent area. Bright boys.

'Two more of my pupils, John Taverner and Howard Shelley, are now well known musicians. At Highgate, all available money went on music, very little on art. The

102

modern side was run by a left-winger called Thomas Fox. He would get off the bus every morning and walk in through the school gates reading a book and shaving. Robert Atkins, who never seemed to me very bright, became a cabinet minister.'

John Coombes, the housemaster Kyffin had asked, unsuccessfully, to administer corporal punishment, recalled: 'Kyffin was a wonderful teacher to any boy who had talent. If they had no talent he did not bother with them. One of the more talented boys painted a mural of a fishing village, which covered the art room attic walls and ceilings. It was very good.'

Kyffin always recalled his pupils with pleasure.

Anthony Howard, CBE, a distinguished biographer and one of the country's leading political journalists, was a pupil of Kyffin's in the junior school. 'His closest friend was a boy called Cohen,' Kyffin recalled. 'They used to argue endlessly. I remember, too, that Howard's short trousers were a damn sight longer than anyone else's. His father was Vicar of Highgate.'

Howard remembered Kyffin with warmth: 'I must have been his worst pupil, never having had the slightest talent for drawing or painting. With his moustachios and ample fair facial hair, he struck us all as a very exotic character bringing a breath of fresh air into the rather stale and sterile wartime air of that institution.

'I remember him coming to tea in the vicarage at Highgate on VE DAY in 1945. There had been a victory service in the forecourt of Highgate School and I suppose my father, a very hospitable man, must have seen him there and asked him to come along. I remember I was slightly taken aback. He had not banished me from his art class, as a later master at Westminster did, but I was only too aware of my maladroit efforts in the subjects which he taught. He was, however, charm itself, and no reference at all was made to my being a far from satisfactory pupil.

'I think the general view in the school was that he was a slightly eccentric figure, but this was at the start of a very long career at Highgate and I have no doubt that by the end of it he had become an icon. By the end of the war most of the masters were in their dotage and as a youthful member of the staff he was pretty exceptional.'

Kyffin would go to enormous lengths to provide facilities for his boys.

Coombes recalled: 'He felt that if we were to be a proper public school we should have a base for sketching in Snowdonia and adventure holidays. He had a friend, Sandy Learmouth, who owned a house and outbuildings in Cwm Pennant, and he persuaded the Head to buy it, and Sandy to sell it, for £500.'

At the time of writing, the school still used the house. In retirement, in Betws Garmon, Coombes ran it.

Kyffin was reminded of his efforts to promote sketching among Highgate boys one day when, embarrassingly, he broke all the rules of mountaineering. He was in Bangor on a dull day and the sun suddenly broke through. He thought he would paint in the Glyders and climbed up to the Devil's Kitchen in his ordinary clothes without any equipment.

He was sitting under a rock drawing happily when he saw a Highgate school party, correctly dressed for the mountains, coming towards him.

Coombes remembered other typically Kyffin incidents. 'He had scripted a school concert to raise funds for a new arts building. He was dressed as a Crimean soldier, singing *Goodbye, Dolly Gray* when my mother, sitting in the front row, collapsed. Kyffin jumped from the stage, bundled her into his Volkswagen and took her to hospital; then came back and finished his song as though nothing had happened.

'Another time I was partnering Kyffin in a tennis match. When we lost the first set, six to one, Kyffin said: There is only one thing to do. We must attack and smash them. He certainly smashed them. He hit the next ball out of the court, the school and probably Highgate beyond. We lost that set 6 nil.'

War brought some bizarre masters to the school. Predictably, Kyffin got on well with them, especially the most exotic of all his colleagues, the PT master Prince Fethi Sami. Prince Sami was a member of the Ottoman Dynasty that had ruled Turkey for five hundred years. His family were forced out of Turkey when, with the blessing of Lloyd George, the Greeks landed at Smyrna. The Samis, who were known to be pro-British, were turned out of their palaces by a Turkish mob and forced to flee to the south of France, where Sami became an Olympic standard boxer.

The family did not give up their palace on the shores of the sea of Marmara lightly. As a boy of 13, Sami had been given a rifle and told by his father, Prince Sami Nedjib, to stay at his post until he died. In the event, a British cruiser arrived and took off the family but they had only two hours to pack and could take little with them.

The family loved all things British because they believed

the British were the fairest race on the planet. Sami remembered a British submarine surfacing in the sea of Marmara next to a boat selling water melons. At pistol point, the skipper demanded the whole cargo, which he paid for in gold. The Germans were less well liked, as Kyffin recalled: 'Sami's father, a captain in the Turkish Lancers, was escorting a German officer who was inspecting his troop. The German slapped a soldier whose button was undone. The Prince said: I do not advise you to do that to a Turkish soldier. The German retorted that a German officer was frightened of nothing, and when he saw a second soldier with his belt undone, he punched him in the stomach. But the third soldier he slapped picked up his rifle and shot the German dead.

'When they came to the south of France, the Samis were penniless and lived over a garage. As the Royal Family, they had owned two oil wells, which they rented to an entrepreneur, Nicolai Gulbenkian. When they were deposed, he stole them and became one of the richest men in the world. Gulbenkian wore a rare orchid in his buttonhole which was replaced every day. He had his own specially rebuilt London taxi, which he famously said would turn on a sixpence – whatever that is. Sami loved Anglesey. He said the Menai Strait reminded him of the Bosphorus.'

Other masters Kyffin remembered were Paddy Ardisher, a jade merchant in peacetime, and John Llewelyn Thomas, a wrangler and a very fine mathematician. 'His father, John Thomas, was Queen Victoria's harpist,' said Kyffin. 'Young John was at Harrow with Samuel Hoare, who became a cabinet minister. When Hoare came to Highgate to open the new science building, John, who didn't realise the loud speaker was switched on, said: There's old Sam. As big a bloody fool as ever. It echoed all over the school.

'The school evacuated to Westward Ho but returned just before the V1 raids began. We had a master, Edward Bullen, totally rotund and inevitably known as The Egg. Wherever he went to live he was followed by a flying bomb. He was bombed out of two new houses in Highgate and was bombed finally while conducting a lesson. He was discovered underneath a blackboard wondering how Hitler always knew where he was. He asked me to dinner with another man called Charlie Benson. Sure enough, in the middle of the dinner the sirens went, we heard a flying bomb. Happily it failed to find him and the jinx was broken.'

Despite such colourful colleagues, life at a school was scarcely the milieu for an artist and even leafy Highgate was a poor exchange for the North Wales mountains in which he had rejoiced. How did Kyffin stick it?

'No option,' he said. 'I wasn't selling pictures. I would rather have taught in an art school because there were girls on the staff in such places. I tried every art school in Britain but none would have me. Times were changing, a new fashion was coming in and I was not wanted because I could draw.'

Nevertheless, after two years of teaching, the need for time to paint became unbearable. When he explained he would have to leave Highgate, headmaster Bell asked: 'Do you have a father who can give you a private income?' Kyffin admitted he had not.

'Then you are an idiot to think of giving up an income.

Why not get a friend to share the job?'

Kyffin brought in his Slade friend, the brilliant painter William Coles. From then on, Kyffin taught for three days and painted for four but it was not easy.

'My sole income was £200,' he said. 'I had not only to live on that: I had to buy paint. My salary went up with time but when I left 27 years later in 1973 I was getting only £1,900 a year as senior arts master. By that time I was selling a few pictures. But the early years were rough. I used to gamble in a second-hand bookshop in Highgate village. Twice a week in the evenings, after the shop closed, all the runners – the men who bought books to sell them on again – assembled and the two rogues who ran it organised gambling sessions. I used to play table tennis there and stay on to gamble. I wouldn't play poker but I knew if I stuck to Rummy I would win two shillings. That was enough to have an omelette and chips at a cafe on Highgate Hill. I couldn't eat in my lodgings. My landlady was blind and couldn't really manage the cooking. She would give me breakfast but I remember once the kippers were cooked in the newspaper they had been wrapped in at the shop.'

Kyffin was poor in the way few people are today. Many of his works were snowscapes. Not from choice. Flake White is the cheapest oil paint. But he insisted: 'The extraordinary thing is that I never worried about not having enough money, although I am a terrible worrier and, like my mother, perpetually filled with apprehension.

'The school was endlessly good to me. When I left in 1973 I was succeeded by a man the new headmaster, Alfred Boulton, allowed me to choose myself. It happened like this. The Keeper of the Royal Academy, Peter Greenham, had been at school with Boulton. I asked Peter for someone for Highgate and he produced Gordon Tweedsdale. When I met Tweedsdale at the school gate, he was wearing a magenta suit with an emerald green lining. I thought, Oh my God, what will Fred say? In the event, Alfred took a liking to him and he was an absolutely howling success. Far better than me. He wasn't mixed up with a desire to be a painter. He had time for all the little perishers and, what is more, he had a wife who did pottery. A boy came to see me years later. He told me that Gordon Tweedsdale had the most successful department in the school.'

Kyffin was also fortunate in the picture framer he found about the same time. Robert Siole was one of the finest framers in Europe. Siole was not his real name. He was C L Roberts but took the name Siole because it sounded French and was good for trade. He was, in fact, Liverpool Welsh and a man of many parts. He had been a pilot in the Royal Flying Corps in World War 1. He was shot down over enemy lines and taken prisoner. While in the camp, he and some fellow prisoners worked up an act as chorus girls. They became so good at it that when they came home they auditioned for the Windmill Theatre.

'Later he met and married Annette Mills, who was to go on to international fame as the creator of the TV puppet, Muffin the Mule. With Annette, he worked up a speciality dancing act and, according to the poet John Ormond, they were responsible for introducing the Charleston to Britain. Roberts had seen it in South America when he toured there in the twenties.

'After he and Annette divorced, he took a job driving a delivery van. Asked to deliver some frames to the Tate one day, he decided he could do a better framing job himself and became a frame designer. He designed frames for all my exhibitions. Indeed, he died the day after setting one up.'

Roberts knew everyone in London. One day he took Kyffin to a bohemian haunt, Chez Kristof on the corner of St Alban's Grove, Kensington. It had been opened by a Polish Prince, Kristof Woroniecki, who had come to Britain to fight with the Polish army and married a beautiful British girl, to whom Kyffin was introduced.

To his astonishment, he discovered she was the daughter of his cousins, the Williamses of Parys Mountain. Her name was Julia and she told him that the last of the Parys Mountain money had gone into the restaurant. As they became more friendly, she confessed: 'I am not sure if I am a blood relation of yours because I do not know if Hwfa Williams was my grandfather or whether it was the Prince of Wales.

'I think it more likely that it was the Prince. He was a frequent visitor to our home on Anglesey, Craig y Don. He came incognito by boat from Bangor, down a road which is still known locally as the Prince's Drive. He was never named in conversation. He was called the Other Man.'

Forty years later, in 1998, the Princess, still a deeply attractive woman, recalled with great fondness the young artist she had met: 'He was charming but deeply combative. I think he hated authority as represented by the Arts Council. He was convinced that people were against him but I know that was not true. Everyone who met him was convinced he had a great talent.'

He prized eccentrics like his Shrewsbury school fellow, Sir

Wynne Cemlyn-Jones of Penmaenmawr, whose portrait he painted in 1952 when he was president of Anglesey Community Council. One day in London Sir Wynne decided to learn to drive. Eschewing an instructor, he drove to the Mall where the traffic was less dense. To his horror, he saw the king and queen approaching in a car from which the Royal Standard fluttered. A loyal subject, he took his hand off the wheel to raise his hat. His car swerved and hit the royal car a glancing blow. Sir Cemlyn never drove again.

Another remarkable friend was Richard Hughes, genius, a schoolmaster's son from Talwrn, on Anglesey. Hughes had been taken up by a local landowner whom he had impressed as a schoolboy by making 200 rabbit hutches in three days. The landowner helped him get a scholarship to Liverpool University where he read naval architecture. Hughes qualified just as the depression hit Britain. Nothing daunted, he headed first for the south of France and then Vienna, where he lived by drawing caricatures. He became so proficient that when he came back to Britain, he was instantly hired to draw a weekly cartoon for *Everyman* magazine. He turned down an offer to do a daily cartoon on a national daily paper because it would have been too tying.

In her nineties, living in Paris and enjoying an international reputation as a maker of collages, his widow Elrika remembered him fondly: 'It was like living on a volcano. He wore a Tyrolean cape and hat, had a black beard and eyes that forever twinkled with excitement.'

Hughes's greatest achievement came after the war when he became interested in water sculpture. He designed the fountain that was the most talked about feature of the Festival of Britain in 1951. He designed similar water features for Liverpool, Grimsby and Basildon New Town. Liverpool's is still there; Grimsby's was destroyed by the council for political reasons; and Basildon's, his finest, was never built through lack of funds.

Elrika remembers Kyffin mainly for his appetite. 'He was always hungry. I don't think he ate very often but Richard was a great admirer of his talent and was always ready to share a meal.'

Two more friends at this time were Diana Armfield RA, RWS, and her partner Bernard Dunston, RA. At her home in Bala, Diana remembered Kyffin as a regular supper guest in the late 1950s and early sixties: 'Our three sons aged five and upwards ate with us as a matter of course. They sat through many small dinner parties of varying interest for them, but they usually slipped away at the end of the meal to get on with their own occupations.

'On Kyffin evenings they seldom budged but sat there through the general conversation to await the next anecdote from Kyffin. There might be two following hard upon each other, one employing a Welsh accent, then perhaps a gap followed by another and so it went on all through the evening. All three of them still ask after him after all these years.

'The scope of the anecdotes was wide, ranging from a near sale at a gallery, baulked when the client fell down dead as she went to sign her cheque; a battle over a tree obscuring his light; a recurring macaroni cheese; the strange attitudes of family and friends; and the outrageous behaviour of various officials in the art world. Perhaps the most relished were the ghost episodes set in Wales.

'Most anecdotes tended to show him in some way as the victim, but for many years this only made the humour more vivid and his expression remained one of affectionate well being. He is, of course, the most marvellous mimic.

'But as well as these wonderful flights of language, we knew him as an artist deeply concerned about the state of the art world in this country. We had many serious discussions on the topic. We also remember his loyalty to other artists and others, not necessarily artists, with whom he felt sympathy.

'Latterly, perhaps due to the diabetes or the epilepsy or perhaps because the official power in the art world shifted further against him, we sometimes felt the humour was no longer working for him as a needed safety valve, almost increasing his suffering as he related the latest iniquities, though always in wonderful, extravagant language.

'We never failed to realise that the splendid entertainment which we enjoyed did carry a grain of anxiety. But the telling seemed to leave him stimulated and happy. Kyffin had such a courteous, strong, social sense that, should a guest be introduced in our circle, he immediately lightened the note. What a friend to have!'

Kyffin certainly had a longer dining-out list than most. In his eighties, the word had only to get about that he was under the weather and well-upholstered ladies bearing chicken casseroles virtually queued to feed him. Some had been looking after him since his days at Highgate.

Chief among these, and loyal until his death, were three beauties, Annwen Williams, Greta Williams and Valerie Price, who were known to the London Welsh as the Three

Graces. So solicitous were they for his well being that they refused to cooperate in this biography in case it upset him – even though the book was his idea.

'I don't remember how I came across them,' said Kyffin. 'It might have been through Michael Wynne Williams, who married Valerie, or it might have been through Bengy Carey-Evans, Lloyd George's grandson, who married Annwen.

'When I met the girls they were already engaged and living in a house in Hampstead. Annwen was a model, Greta was going to be a teacher and Val was training to be a physiotherapist. They were very beautiful and so kind. I could go over to them at any time and they would rustle up a meal for me. I was always in favour of having a free meal so I saw them quite often. I painted Annwen. I was very fond of her. A hell of a lot of people were but Bengy was on the scene.'

The three were not only beautiful and kind: they were also multi-talented.

Valerie Wynne Williams has been, in turn, a physiotherapist, teacher, magazine editor, TV presenter, radio interviewer, interior designer, actress, theatre director, Plaid Cymru candidate and quarry manager.

In a radio interview some years ago, she told me: 'I went to London as a little country girl from South Wales and was amazed to find there were more trees there than there were at home. We were very good little girls. Annwen refused to model swimsuits in case it upset people in her home village of Llanerchymedd (Anglesey). We were very hospitable. Kyffin often came in for a meal. The flat was on the edge of Hampstead Heath and Kyffin was teaching at Highgate so it was handy. It was a small flat. It only had two bedrooms and it was filled with his paintings. When I left to get married to Michael and help him run the family business at the Dorothea Quarry, Kyffin asked me whether, as a wedding present, I would like him to paint my portrait or choose one of his other paintings. There was a marvellous portrait of Richard Hughes and I chose that.

'Another visitor to our flat was the poet and painter David Jones. I had interviewed him and we had been in correspondence in *The Times*. We invited him to a Plaid Cymru party but he was something of a recluse and he made an excuse. However, we corresponded further and in time he came round. From then on he was a regular visitor. Always with the same taxi, which he kept no matter how long he stayed. We tried to get him to pay it off and get another when he was ready to leave but he said he needed to have familiar things around him. We became very close. His painting of me as Aphrodite was shown at the Tate Gallery. I have it now with my Kyffin. My most treasured possessions.'

Greta (now Greta Berry) once told me that David Jones was obsessed with Valerie but it was Kyffin's paintings that adorned the flat. 'We had dozens of them stacked against the walls. The one I remember best was a huge mountainscape in my bedroom. It was the first thing I saw when I woke in the mornings. It was marvellous but it made me homesick. We all three of us mothered him and fed him at every possible opportunity. He didn't look as though he was eating regularly.'

Rosalie Sinclair, his friend from the Slade, was shocked when she visited him in London: 'His lodgings were always extremely modest. He had no one to cook or clean for him. He didn't drink, of course. In fact, he kept himself very much to himself and was totally absorbed in his painting.'

That was not quite true. Although the least domesticated of men, he had ways of keeping his studio clean. Years later he admitted: 'I tried wherever possible to use German *au pair* girls as models. I discovered they had a passion for tidiness. When they came to the studio for a sitting the first thing they would do was clean it up.

'In those days I used to wander about a lot down by the Thames, painting. It was an odd life. William Coles, who was teaching with me, also shared my lodgings at 12 Bisham Gardens. He had plenty of money and was extremely idle. Sometimes he wouldn't get up in the morning and I had to start the lessons off. He got on terribly well with the girls. I didn't. I suppose because, basically, I am a melancholic. I am seldom happy but I hide it by being a clown.'

Curiously, none of the girls with whom Kyffin claimed he was in love as a young man was aware of it. Interviewed as old ladies, they almost all affected surprise when they were told how he had felt. It could be, of course, that they were accomplished actresses. Or perhaps Kyffin's courting techniques were so elliptical as to be invisible.

That was certainly not true of Coles. Perhaps knowingly, he was almost a caricature, as so many art students in the forties were, of the painter Strickland in Somerset Maugham's novel *The Moon and Sixpence*.

In Kyffin's second volume of autobiography, *A Wider Sky*, after discreetly altering his name to Maurice Wood, Kyffin told how Coles had visited Frank Welby, another artist and mutual friend, in Paris. When he arrived at his flat, the door was opened by Welby's mistress, a voluptuous milliner called Suzy. She told him that Welby was visiting England. By the time he returned, Coles had replaced him in Suzy's bed. Astonishingly, Welby accepted the situation. He made up a bed in the kitchen and became both cuckold and cook.

Coles was capable of even greater treachery. As Kyffin wrote: 'Suzy discovered she was pregnant... he (Coles) realised that for the first time in his life he was not in control of a situation and his money could not buy his way out of it. Terrified, he returned to Torquay where his father agreed to stop his allowance so that Suzy could not benefit from the family wealth. Many were the times Suzy telephoned me from Paris... Many times she was in tears as she cried into the telephone: I hate him, I hate him, but oh, what a lover...'

Welby offered to marry Suzy and adopt Coles's baby but she refused.

Kyffin was clearly shocked by his friend. He admitted: 'I saw little of Coles when he returned. He said I must never mention anything about Suzy in Paris. I tried to get in touch with him several times when I was writing *A Wider Sky*. I didn't get a reply so I assumed he was dead. Then at my show in the Thackeray in 1998 I saw an entry in the Remarks Book which read: I am William Coles's sister. The trouble with Coles was that he had this immense talent, and he taught me more than anyone ever did, but he had no stamina, no strength, to see a picture through. I thought then it was laziness but I think now it was his heart.

'He was one of those absolutely brilliant people who die unknown. He taught me to look at everything. To work out the colour of a puddle, what colour the sun was, shining on a wet roof. He told me everything is colour. He drew beautifully but he just had not got the stamina.

'He used to come and stay at home. My mother couldn't stand him because he wouldn't lift a finger. He was totally self absorbed.'

Coles's painting talent was not the only thing Kyffin envied about his friend. There was that success with girls. He recalled: 'He was so arrogant and the girls worshipped him for it. In our lodgings he was always being rung up by girls who had fallen in love with him. I remember one literally going mad on the phone. She insisted he was there when he wasn't. She got more and more agitated until I put the phone down. She was subsequently found wandering on Hampstead Heath and was incarcerated in Colney Hatch lunatic asylum.'

It must have been very provoking for Kyffin whose own love life was constantly being shipwrecked.

'In life drawing classes at the Slade we had a new pose every month and you had to draw lots for an easel,' Kyffin remembered. 'William (Coles) never used to come in time for the draw. He would stroll in at half past ten because he knew that lots of girls would offer him their easels. He would never even say thank you. I remember a visit to Ffestiniog with William and another friend, Tom Griffiths, where he painted lots of lovely paintings. Then he went off to Paris and faded out of our lives. William never had an exhibition, though he was streets ahead of almost everyone, in a different class altogether. But he wasn't totally obsessed and without that it doesn't work.

'We went to the Scilly Isles on a painting holiday and he didn't paint a single picture. When we got back I composed a limerick for him:

There was a young artist called Willy
Went to paint in the Island of Scilly
He thought it more fun
Just to lie in the sun
So the output of Willy was nilly.'

Chapter seven

Slowly Kyffin's pictures began to sell but there were still disastrous interludes. In the late forties, he was invited to have an exhibition in Terry Hebberd's gallery in a music shop in Caernarfon. A Blaenau Ffestiniog woman saw a painting she liked. She asked the price, and when Hebberd told her £60, she said: 'I cannot afford that but I must have it.' She sat down and had just started to write a cheque when she dropped dead. The excitement of spending so much on a picture had been too much for her.

On another occasion in a gallery in the National Museum of Wales, Kyffin noticed with horror that someone had scribbled in biro over one of his pictures. His was the only picture in the gallery that had not been glazed.

He entered a competition to mark the fiftieth anniversary of the Football Association. The entries, paintings of footballers, were to be exhibited in Londonderry House in London's Park Lane. Kyffin entered a painting of one of his Highgate schoolboys in his house colours. Although it did not win a prize, it was bought by the Contemporary Arts Society and presented to the Glynn Vivian Art Gallery in Swansea.

Subsequently, the director of the gallery loaned the picture to a local mental home. A woman inmate attacked the picture with a knife and severed the head from the body. The director asked whether Kyffin could restore it if he had the canvas relined. Kyffin painted in a new head. His bill read:

'To restoring a footballer's head: £120. To repairing footballer's shorts: £50.'

Mrs Nancy Thomas of Aberaeron, Cardiganshire, bought an inoffensive painting of cottages at Llandonna (Anglesey). 'One day I was in the studio and I got a call,' Kyffin remembered. 'A voice said: My name is Annie Williams. I am speaking on behalf of Mrs Nancy Thomas. A terrible thing has happened. Her husband came home from work, saw your painting on the wall, pulled out a revolver and shot himself dead in front of it. And the picture is covered in blood. Will you take the blood off? Little wonder I got the reputation of being the most lethal painter in Britain.

'My pictures got stolen as well. I had a very big picture, 30 inches by 50, of Harlech, which was stolen from the common room in UCW, Swansea, and 30 were stolen from my studio without me knowing it. Not surprising I suppose: I had 500 at the time.'

In 1980, there was a retrospective exhibition of privately-owned paintings by Kyffin. A few weeks after they were returned, a letter came from a Lady Robinson in Northampton accusing the organisers of damaging a work that she had loaned. The organisers contacted Kyffin who offered to collect the painting and restore it free of charge. The organisers were amazed at her solicitor's reply. They wrote: 'Our client would prefer to have the work done professionally.'

Apart from part-time teaching and intermittent sales, Kyffin's source of income was buying and selling pictures. His mother hit the roof when he paid £14 for a picture he believed to be a Richard Wilson at a junk shop in Chester.

No one in London would accept his attribution. Nevertheless Kyffin took the painting to William Constable, the director of the Boston Fine Arts Museum who had just written the definitive work on Wilson. He recognised it at once. 'Ah, the missing Wilson,' he said. 'I was looking for it for my book.' He wrote about the newly discovered Wilson in *The Burlington Magazine* and a dealer snapped it up.

Other paintings Kyffin had to sell included those he had inherited from his cousins, the Ramsays. 'There was a lovely big painting by Marco Ricci of some Roman ruins,' he recalls. 'I loved it but I had bills outstanding for paints and canvas. I sold it to a friend, Jack Baer, who had the Hazlitt Gallery, and he sold it on to a big Italian collection where it still hangs.'

Although it had upset Rosalie Sinclair, a certain amount of squalor is to be expected at the lodgings of an up-and-coming young artist, but despite the ministrations of German *au pairs*, Kyffin's home in Bisham Gardens exceeded the acceptable amount by a wide margin. The green hall, the dirt-encrusted paintings, even the dung-brown painted woodwork, could be overlooked. Not so the smells. Part cat, part dog, part cabbage, they merged with the overwhelming odour of his landlady's, Miss Mary Josling's, stockpot, which was forever a-bubble. It was the stockpot that drove him to find a new home. It was then, he later insisted, that he began to take himself seriously as a painter: 'It was only when I had nowhere to paint that I realised how hooked I had become. I was going round knocking on doors to find a studio but they were all occupied by old women who weren't painters at all. It made me very angry.'

Leila Troup offered to help. She had a friend who had married a diplomat. They said Kyffin could have a room in their basement in St John's Wood, so he moved in, but quickly regretted it.

He told me:

> I was a sort of dogsbody. I had to pay my rent; I had to stoke the boiler; I had to mow the lawn; I had to trim the vine; I had to babysit; I had to produce pictures for their house; I had to clear the children's toffee papers. I was at their beck and call, their tame artist, and still they complained.
>
> I think the trouble was that I did not pay enough attention to the wife and she resented it. She was very pretty and she liked men to flutter around. But I was a friend of her friend and it would have been quite wrong to dance attendance.
>
> She suddenly started hating me. I had never been really hated before. Every time she spoke to me her face became creased. Both of them did everything they could to get me to go. Once I was ordered up to their living room. She was knitting. Her husband told me to sit down. He had been given orders, I think. He was a nice chap, basically. He said 'Now Taff, you haven't been pulling your weight you know.' I went through the list of my tasks. He shook his head: 'You haven't been picking up many toffee papers in the yard and we have all got to pull our weight. If I were in your place I know I'd be an A1 tenant. I am afraid you only add up to a Beta minus.'
>
> Finally, I got a note to say that I had insulted their daily. The daily was unaware of this when I asked her about it, but I put all my pictures into a basement at Highgate school and moved in with another painter, Fred Uhlman, and his wife. When I wrote *Across the Straits* I

put in a bit about these people although I changed the name.

About five years after the book came out I got a letter from the diplomat's wife saying how appalled she was to read the book. She was furious and demanded I take immediate steps to remove all the paintings I'd given them when I lived in the house. These included a life sized portrait of their son. I could have sent in a bill for the painting for about £15,000 but I just burned the letter.

Manfred and Diana Uhlman were loyal friends in Kyffin's London days of poverty. Diana was the sister of the second Lord Croft, of Croft Castle in Dorset, where her family had lived since the fourteenth century. She was educated at Malvern School for Girls and 'finished' in Paris and Florence, and she had been presented at court. Her father, Sir Henry Page Croft, Bart., was Conservative MP for Christchurch. She rebelled against her background and her father was furious when she sent her brother Michael, then at Eton, a copy of Aldous Huxley's *Brave New World*. When, in London in 1936, she greeted the Jarrow hunger marchers, he was apoplectic.

But much worse was to come. On holiday in Spain she met Manfred, a German-Jewish refugee who had been a lawyer for the German Social Democratic Party. He had escaped from Germany in 1933, the day before he was due to be sent to a concentration camp. He had worked, unsuccessfully, in Paris as a journalist, picture dealer, painter and purveyor of tropical fish.

They made an unlikely couple: she, tall, graceful, aristocratic and beautiful; he 4ft 10ins and ugly. But Manfred fell madly in love. When Diana returned to England, all he knew of her was the name of her bank.

He wrote to every branch in Britain until at last he tracked her down. He came to England and Diana, impressed by his devotion and no doubt striking a blow for the workers, agreed to marry him. Once again, her father was furious. He summoned Uhlman to his office in the House of Commons. It was a frustrating meeting. Uhlman had no English, Sir Henry had no German. A fellow MP had to translate the row that followed.

Sir Henry informed Uhlman that he did not approve of his daughter marrying a penniless Jew – and, almost as bad, an artist. He said on no account was the marriage to take place, but the couple were married in Chelsea in 1936 and remained close and happy for half a century.

In 1938, Diana formed the Freier Deutscher Kulturbund (an artists' refugee committee). It supported artists who had fled from Austria, Germany and occupied Czechoslovakia. In all, it brought forty artists to England, including Oskar Kokoschka, and the Uhlman house in Hampstead, as well as being a refuge for Kyffin, became a meeting place for exiles. A portrait of Diana's brother, later the second Lord Croft, was Kokoschka's first commission.

The war brought contrasting fortunes for Diana's family. Her father was appointed joint Under Secretary of State for War and vice-president of the Army Council and created a peer. Fred was interned in the Isle of Man as an enemy alien.

In Douglas, he shared a house with two eccentrics. One, a professor of pure mathematics, believed he was a Dachshund. The other, the Dadaist Kurt Schwitters, believed he was an Alsatian. Occasionally they would meet on the landing and bark at each other.

Kyffin painted a portrait of Uhlman and presented it to the National Library of Wales. Their friendship grew but as

Uhlman began to make his name, he used Kyffin – whom he always called 'Coffin' – unscrupulously.

Kyffin remembered: 'He used to ring me up occasionally and say, 'Coffin, my dear, can you bring me some of your drawings of Wales? I wish to do some paintings of Wales.' I would bring him down a dozen drawings and he would copy them and sell them for quite a lot of money. I couldn't make any money at all. In fact, one of his paintings of a windmill at Llanerchymedd, which he did from a drawing of mine, is in the national collection.'

Kyffin was extremely cross to read a *Daily Telegraph* review of an early exhibition he shared with Uhlman and Jonah Jones in Portmeirion. It read: 'Williams has been doing some paintings in Uhlman country.'

After Uhlman moved to Croft Castle, where he was to spend the rest of his life, they saw less of each other. So little, indeed, that Uhlman once wrote to ask if Kyffin were dead.

In reply, Kyffin sent off one of his impromptu rhymes:

A man from Penrhyndeudraeth said
That Fred was dead.
No, indeed he is not, I said,
He has merely gone right off his head
And taken to his bed,
In the Croft Castle potting shed.

Sadly, Uhlman died six months later in 1983. Diana spent the rest of her life at the castle, restoring the gardens. She prevented the National Trust, which took it over, from building a car park on the ruins of a Tudor wing. Instead, with her bare hands, she cleared the area of tons of bricks and rubble and established a garden stocked with ancient plants. She also created an ornamental garden and planted a small vineyard. Another of her ideas was for a 'lending library' for works of art that people could borrow and, if they wished, buy at a reduced price. She died in November 1999, still working and plotting at the age of 87, having helped her brother restore the castle.

In the four days each week he had free from teaching at Highgate, Kyffin tried to paint two pictures – this at a time when he could hardly afford paint and in addition was deeply worried at the deteriorating mental state of his mother:

> I came home one Christmas and found her in a terrible state. She had all the family silver out. She insisted some had been stolen and all night she moaned and went on counting and counting each piece over and over. I could do nothing with her.
>
> She gradually got worse and worse until the doctor came and said she would have to go to a mental home. He begged me not to get Dick back because he knew she liked Dick and in these cases people tend to destroy the thing they love most. So we had to keep Dick out of it. Finally, they came to take her away and it was terrible. She broke away and ran down the lane with these people hunting after her. They caught her in a rick yard. It was absolute hell. I was there for a whole week trying to help. In the end I had to send for Dick. We thought the only thing to do was to buy a small house for her on Anglesey and she went to live there.
>
> She was still very protective of Dick. There was this business of Dick's holiday abroad. She was contemptuous. 'How can he go abroad with no one to look after him?' she said. I said that I went abroad and she said, 'It's different for you.'

I didn't point out that I was an epileptic but there was nothing wrong with Dick.

In the end I said to him, 'Look, tell me where you want to go and I will take you.' He said he would like to go to Scotland. It was unwise. The further north we got the more insecure he became, worrying where he would be sleeping that night. He became very strange. At Ullapool he flipped and I knew I had to get him back to Chester.

The next year I took him to Ireland to stay with one of my pupils. We had no sooner got there than a telegram came from my mother saying she was in hospital with a broken arm and wanted us home. We got home and found she hadn't broken her arm: she just wanted to see Dick.

By this time he was getting not to like her. It ended by her suddenly realising towards the end of her life that I actually cared for her more than he did. This was a terrible blow for her. When she was living in Gadlys, the house we got for her, she used to go out at night and sleep under the hedges. She would turn up at Treffos, the old family home, the next morning covered in leaves and twigs. She was very unhappy. We are an extraordinary family. I have never known what it is to be happy. But I am better off than she was. She thought all her apprehensions were valid. I always question mine. She desperately didn't want to be a burden but her apprehension was a terrible strain. I sensed she thought she was inferior. She was always terribly worried what people thought about her. She used to get furious because I wanted to paint on Sundays. I was about forty at the time.

Outside his family, people were beginning to appreciate his work. In 1946, his first picture was accepted by the Royal

128

Academy but he had less success when he tried to get dealers interested in his work. He was astonished how rude they could be and at the insulting things they said. One gallery owner described him as 'a poor imitator of Cezanne', another claimed he was far too like Camille Pissarro. Yet another gallery owner said, 'For God's sake, hide them. Someone may come in.'

The only good-mannered reception he got was from Colonel Beddington in Wildenstein's. Kyffin recalled: 'The colonel's real name was Moses. When he joined the cavalry he thought it wiser to change his name. The first morning he went into the officers' mess under his new name there was a huge notice that said: The Lord said unto Moses, Good Morning, Mr Beddington.

'Despite ribbing like this, he was a very nice man. He said: Mr Williams, I am going to pay you a compliment and compare your work with Daumier. Otherwise everywhere I went I got a flea in my ear. Fortunately my reports at Shrewsbury had been so uniformly awful I had learnt to put up with such treatment. Rough handling by critics does not disturb me. I knew worse at school. The problem was that in the West End you cannot get a show without influence and in 1946 I had none.'

Writing of Kyffin's life, it is tempting to see a guiding hand gently pushing him, not always willingly, to his present eminence as the greatest Welsh artist. As a boy out hunting, he met Ernest Naish, who taught him to paint. No sooner had an army doctor started him thinking about becoming an artist than he met Gwyneth, the lovely land girl who got him into the Slade. A sympathetic headmaster allowed him to work part-time and paint the rest of the week.

Soon, the guiding hand was to propel into his path the man who was to launch him on his career proper.

Ralph Edwards was a polymath. An irascible little man, plagued with a painful duodenal ulcer, he was a farmer's son from South Wales. He is still, long after his death, recognised as the greatest expert on English furniture in the world. He was the author of the standard work on the subject.

Modern Wales can be divided into two periods: Before and After Saunders Lewis. That Liverpool-born, Welsh minister's son had ambitions to be a poet. In Paris, in the 1920s, he fell in with the expatriate Irish community. He complained to Synge, the playwright, that he could find no subject for his muse. Synge advised him to go home and write about the Welsh struggle for freedom. 'But they aren't struggling,' objected Lewis. 'Then go home and start a struggle,' Synge advised. Lewis took Synge's advice and virtually invented Welsh Nationalism, single-handed.

In the sixties he made an inflammatory broadcast on BBC Wales calling on the young men of Wales to rise and shake off their oppressors, and a new Wales was born. Until then, Wales had been ruled unofficially by the London Welsh, among whom Ralph Edwards reigned supreme. He met Kyffin on the recommendation of Professor Schwabe, whom he had consulted about young Welsh artists of promise.

Edwards liked what he saw at the artist's studio. He bought two pictures, one for himself and one for the Contemporary Arts Society of Wales, for which he was a talent spotter. He also recommended the young unknown to his friends, among them Captain Geoffrey Crawshay, a giant of a man who bought two pictures and invited Kyffin to his annual grouse shoot on the slopes of Plynlimmon. This was not so much a shoot as an annual gathering of Welshmen from all walks of life and considerable eminence who between them controlled Wales. The original Taffia.

Geoffrey Crawshay was in his heyday one of the finest shots in Britain but the same could not be said for some of his guests. They included architects, senior policemen, bards, judges and serviceman, and their power was considerable. One day Kyffin and two other guns who comprised the shoot 'art committee' were in a car driven by a local man, Duodenal Jenkins. It was the sort of day Kyffin always hoped for – grey and misty when shooting would be abandoned and the arts committee could drive to Gregynog to see the remarkable collection there of art, owned by the two spinster sisters Gwendoline and Margaret Davies. The paintings were mostly French impressionists: Monet, Pissarro, Cezanne, Van Gogh, Gauguin and Renoir. There was sculpture by Rodin and other paintings by Augustus John, Sickert and many more.

As they anticipated the joys to come, the talk turned to the future of the collection. The arts committee decided that when the sisters died their collection must go to the National Gallery of Wales, although there was strong interest from other UK galleries. The committee won and the paintings are now housed in their own magnificent wing of the National Gallery of Wales in Cardiff.

Ralph Edwards's son is Nicholas Edwards, the former Welsh Secretary and now Lord Crickhowell. At the family home in the Black Mountains, he told me about the shoot: 'My father and mother lived on Chiswick Mall in London when Kyffin was teaching at Highgate. They all used to go up to this extraordinary shoot. There was a teetotal hotel in Llandinam owned by Lord Davies, who abominated liquor in any form. Lord Davies even controlled the time the local people went to bed by switching off the electrical supply to the whole village.

'The shoot was an annual event at which the social chit-chat was about Wales and its politics and art. It was a great deal more important than the shooting. Geoffrey had been a very great shot. He once told me that in his heyday when he was one of the dozen best shots in the country, he would shoot fifty thousand cartridges a year. But he was very badly injured in the First World War and could no longer bend his right arm. He had a special gun made which he threw up with his left hand and, even then, he was still able to out-shoot most people.

'His guests at the annual shoot, to which Kyffin was invited, were all prominent people in Welsh life, involved in the National Museum and suchlike. It did Kyffin no harm to know them.'

Among the people Kyffin met on the shoot were Sir Wynne Cemlyn-Jones, Sir Wynn Wheldon and his son Huw (who was to rise to eminence in the BBC) and the Reverend Twm Hollingworth, an East End vicar with a wonderful voice.

Crawshay took over the teetotal hotel, the Red Lion, and for the duration of the shoot it flowed with beer, and every evening there was a singsong round the piano.

One of the most important pieces of networking Kyffin did was with a director of the National Museum and Gallery of Wales, Sir Leonard Twiston-Davies, whose son Tony later held the same position. But Kyffin's greatest friendship was with his daughter Suzanne, now Suzanne Hunter and an international journalist. At her home in the Bahamas, she remembered how for many years Kyffin kept quiet about his epilepsy:

He used to take me out to dinner (in a very platonic way – though he was always falling in love with people whose portraits he'd painted) but sometimes he'd say, I cannot take you out to dinner tomorrow, I think I am going to have flu. I used to think, why don't you wait until you have actually got flu? But later I discovered that he could feel the epilepsy coming on and, naturally, didn't want to give me a shock.

When I worked for the BBC, the corporation medic Dr Elizabeth Fletcher had a Kyffin on her wall. Kyffin had lodged with her and she told me about the epilepsy, though Kyffin was later to be open about it.

When he did take me out to dinner, he would frighten me to death by collecting me in this large van, big enough to hold his landscapes. I was frightened because it had a rear engine and it appeared as though there was nothing between us and the bus ahead.

He was a terrific companion. Very amusing. Very funny about Highgate School. When required to do a portrait of Guy Fawkes, the boys always did an exact picture of Kyffin, complete with drooping moustaches. He was always having rows with his headmaster who wanted the boys to learn to paint. He reckoned they did not need to learn to draw, but Kyffin was adamant.

He was pretty critical of various presidents of the National Museum but, luckily, much admired my brother Tony and Tim Edwards, Ralph's son. He used to say, At least they know about art.

I think he quarrelled with most of the members of

most of the committees he was on and he had no time for most RAs.

He worried terribly about his brother Dick. He used to despair when they were going on holiday. He would tell me they would reach a likely hotel and Kyffin would suggest they see if it had rooms. Dick usually replied: Don't let's go in. It would be so humiliating if they haven't got rooms and turn us away. Kyffin said they often ended up sleeping in the car.

Lord Crickhowell remembers Kyffin and Suzanne being very close but admitted that Kyffin fell in love with many women in his life. He believed it was his epilepsy that made him decide marriage was not for him. 'Later there were people who would have married him but by then he had taken, I think, a conscious decision not to marry,' he said. 'A deeply susceptible man, Kyffin would rather have been a husband and father than a painter. At best, painting offered a way of escape from his epilepsy. In real life there was no escape.'

As a schoolboy, he recalled Kyffin's many visits to the family home: 'Kyffin became a regular visitor to our home where there was a very great ritual of tea. My father suffered all his life from a duodenal ulcer. His temper only improved after tea about four in the afternoon. Cake and jam and everything. To say that Kyffin came every week would be to exaggerate but he came very often to tea and supper. He became a close friend of mine when I was a schoolboy at Westminster and of my brother Tim. He was always very welcome. He was full of wonderful tales and we were enchanted by them. Kyffin wore venerable corduroy trousers and an artist's jacket and his moustache was even longer than it is now.

'We had a pestilential Jack Russell terrier who once ate the shoulder out of a chinchilla coat of an extremely rich American visitor. On another occasion as we sat at the tea table, he was tugging round Kyffin's leg. When he got up he found the whole of his corduroy trousers to the knee had virtually disappeared.'

The benefits of acquaintance with the Edwards' family far outweighed the sartorial hazards. Crickhowell continued: 'One day, my father, who was on the council of the National Museum of Wales for fifty years, said: Look here, Kyffin, it's time you had a show. He was also a buyer for the Contemporary Arts Society of Wales and very much in the way of encouraging young artists. He persuaded Byam Shaw, the senior partner at the fine art dealers Colnaghi's, to put on an exhibition by Kyffin in the gallery. It was rather an unusual show for Colnaghi, which specialised in old master prints and drawings, but nevertheless Kyffin had his first one-man show at Colnaghi's in Old Bond Street.'

Kyffin recalled with gratitude how Shaw and another dealer called Tom Baskett came to see his work. In all, the gallery put on three of his shows, including one of his drawings, which he shared with Augustus John and Muirhead Bone.

Although his relations with Colnaghi were harmonious they would never show his portraits. Once again, Ralph Edwards used his influence to put Kyffin in touch with the Leicester Galleries. The Galleries agreed to put him in a show with two young fashionable artists, Anthony Fry and Ronald Searle. A friend warned him that the art world was behind them and they would be praised at his expense. So it proved.

Eric Newton, whom Kyffin believed to be the best art critic in London, wrote: 'Mr Fry at 30 is a more sensitive artist than Mr Williams at 40, whose ponderous, unimaginative and insensitive works are shown in the adjoining gallery.'

Neville Wallace wrote in *The Observer:* 'What bad luck for the steady going Mr Williams to be sandwiched between the genius of Mr Fry and Mr Searle.'

The most cruel of all the critics was Nigel Gosling, who wrote three words in the *Sunday Times,* 'Herman and Soda', implying that Kyffin was a pale imitation of Joseph Herman.

It is said that artists are not affected by their critics. Strange, then, that forty years later Kyffin could quote all three verbatim. He was most upset by Gosling's cruel jibe. At that time he had never seen Herman's work and still insisted to his dying day that the only thing they had in common was that they both painted with black ink.

There were more perceptive critics. In the *Liverpool Daily Post,* Elizabeth Coxhead, after visiting one of his thirty one-man exhibitions, wrote: 'His work is not much bought by the public and he is glad to eke out the money he gets from his paintings by working as a schoolmaster. He says ruefully, "I don't paint what people want." The fact is that, like all artists of original vision, he is having a long struggle to impose it... His recognition will come not from fashionable people who want something modish to hang on their walls but from climbers and walkers who know the hills as Kyffin knows them.'

How true that turned out to be.

Chapter eight

Kyffin insisted until the end of his life that the Arts Council and the Welsh Arts establishment hated him and his work, and it was true that in later life there were some pretty spectacular quarrels.

Lord Crickhowell agreed: 'I think he was probably right in thinking – if there is such a thing as an arts establishment – that it was against him. The reason was, of course, that he expressed himself strongly. He painted in a traditional style and had very strong views of things that have gone on in the art schools in this country for forty years. With some justice. He was almost intemperate, but absolutely right. Even those students who want to be abstract painters need the basic skills of draughtsmanship. My niece, whom he encouraged very much, went to the *Ecole des Beaux Arts* in Paris. Students there are not allowed to do anything for three years but draw and draw and draw. She painted only after she left.'

It was those strong views that led to disagreements with the Welsh Arts Council. No one knows more about those disagreements than Llion Williams, who retired to Colwyn Bay from his post as director of the North Wales Arts Association. Llion met Kyffin formally when he was appointed in 1974 but he had known him vaguely in London in the fifties when he was a science teacher.

'In those days he sold very little,' Llion told me, 'but he was a great teacher. You only have to look at the list of successful painters he taught. Yet he was never asked to teach in an art school.

'A year after I joined the association, we got the idea of doing an exhibition of crow-stepped gabled houses in North Wales to mark European Architectural Year. We set up a committee and invited Kyffin, who was interested in architecture as art, to act as chairman. We opened it at the National Eisteddfod in Criccieth and I told Kyffin he would have to make the opening speech.

'He was reluctant because he would have to speak in Welsh and he did not think he was sufficiently fluent. I insisted because I knew that was an excuse. I knew that when he went out painting he spoke to farmers in Welsh. In the end he performed the opening ceremony with great success.

'Nine months later he came into my office in Bangor and asked if I knew there was an art gallery in Llandudno. I didn't. But I looked and there it was. A custom built art gallery, rented to Rushworth's music shop, who were using it as a warehouse. I knew it had possibilities but Kyffin wanted it for the Royal Cambrian Academy, of which he was president, so I held back.

'I was delighted when the RCA refused to move there, leaving us with the possibility of developing an independent gallery. I brought a gathering together to look at it and we got working. We set up a council of management and a limited company with charitable status. I was in Cardiff one day when Aneurin Thomas and Peter Jones of the Welsh Arts Council collared me. I hear you are going to put Kyffin on the council of management of your new gallery, one of them said. I said, Of course, why shouldn't I? They said, He is a danger to Welsh art, that man. A bad influence on art in Wales. I said they were entitled to their opinion but we could not leave Kyffin out of the development of a major gallery in North Wales. I just ignored them.

'In the event, we ran into financial difficulties. It was going to cost £250,000 to renovate the building and we were fifty thousand short. The only source of funds was the buildings committee of the Welsh Arts Council. We soon sensed that we would only get help if we got rid of Kyffin. In the end we called their bluff. We went to Cardiff to tell them we couldn't afford to complete the contract. We told them that if they refused help we would hand over the lease to the Arts Council and they would have to run it.

'They realised the political implications. I had already told a lot of people of influence that the Arts Council wanted to run it from Cardiff. That was anathema. So they gave in and gave us the money.

'Our plan for the gallery was to have a balanced programme. We were prepared to push to the frontiers of art with difficult exhibitions so long as the balance was maintained. But that didn't happen. With his enormous knowledge of art, Kyffin was in a position of strength. But Kyffin, Leslie Jones and myself were accused of keeping the gallery back. We resigned.

'Some years ago we put together a retrospective of Kyffin's work and it took us two years to get it off the ground. There was resistance, and since 99 per cent of the works were in private hands, insurance was a great problem. The National Museum is the only gallery in Wales which has a government indemnity so we had to get them on board. Finally they agreed and the exhibition had a critical success.

'The National Museum wanted us to launch it in Turner House but we pointed out that the exhibition was the work of a major artist and it should start in the National Gallery of Wales.

'Until they opened a gallery of Welsh art – another Kyffin suggestion – he was only represented in that gallery by a hopeless example of his work from the late forties. I know he offered two canvasses, free of charge, to take its place but they weren't interested. They even hung one of his paintings in the new refectory. A subsequent director, Colin Ford, was all for accepting Kyffin's offer. A painting, specifically for the gallery, was put aside and kept at Oriel Ynys Môn but it was never collected. Somewhere in middle management he had an enemy. I do not understand it.

'Kyffin put himself in every picture. There are other Welsh painters who are fine craftsmen but they do not seem to love their subjects in the way Kyffin did. He used unusual colours and used them with great subtlety. He was never interested in money. His prices were lower than most. For a good Kyffin oil you paid around £5,000 in Sotheby's, which is chicken feed because there will only ever be one Kyffin. People loved him and will go on buying his works.

'I remember telling Aneurin Thomas, who was chairman of the Welsh Arts Council, that his council was scared Kyffin would start a Welsh school of painting and that would be anathema to the Arts Council because it was promoting the '56 Group' in South Wales. Their paintings could have come from anywhere.

'When you look at a Scottish group, there is a Scottish stamp on their work. Apart from Kyffin, there has never been that national stamp on our painting. I suggested the last thing the Arts Council wanted was a Welsh school of art and he didn't deny it.

'This reaction against Kyffin manifests itself in some strange ways. In 1997, when he was asked to do a master class on TV, there was not an art school that would let its pupils take part.'

Llion Williams maintained that in his day the Arts Council in Wales didn't like successful artists.

'They were running a social service for struggling artists. When Lady Anglesey became chairman of the Arts Council, the director and Peter Jones, the art director, immediately concluded he would influence her because they were friends. Jones thought that in anything to do with art she would be seeking Kyffin's opinion. It was nonsense, of course. She is her own woman with very strong views and opinions.'

Williams also made the point that Kyffin was never asked to take part in any overseas exhibition.

'The art establishment, and I would include in that the National Museum and Art Gallery, never missed an opportunity to stab him in the back. He was put on the art committee but he was a thorn in their side. He would question their purchases. I reckon Kyffin was one of the best art historians in Wales, so well versed in art history he could constructively criticise modern art and show where it had gone wrong. Twenty years ago I commissioned him to give the Ben Bowen annual lecture: Is tradition in danger? It was a cracking speech. He infuriated the establishment because, quite rightly, he criticised all the 'isms'.

'I forget who described art as a passionate mistress but Kyffin committed himself whole-heartedly to her. In his eightieth year he showed me a painting he had done with Crib Goch in the foreground and Snowdon in the distance. It was one of his best. How did he do it?

'That year he had fifty oils in a London exhibition and another forty in Swansea. He had done an oil of the poet R S Thomas which caught the spirit of the man to a T. Quite his best portrait. At 80. It was an incredible talent.'

In fact the talent was recognised a good deal earlier than Kyffin chose to admit. He was one of three Slade students who were chosen as 'promising' and given an exhibition in the Ashmolean.

Early in his career, the Arts Council of Wales clearly shared that view of him. In 1949, they bought a painting and wrote glowingly of its purchase: 'To know him casually one would hardly believe the fire which burns in him, a fire which seems to be nourished equally by a love of the mountains and a love of art. His gift is rather in his sensitivity and imaginative use of tonal arrangement rather than in precise drawing.'

Lord Crickhowell suggested a reason why Kyffin's reputation was confined to Wales: 'The English don't understand us or even recognise we exist. They probably don't recognise the mood that Kyffin expresses whereas Welshmen can hardly wait for the next show. There is no one capable of painting the mood that is Wales better than he.

'He painted the atmosphere of his native land extraordinarily well. The contrasts of light, the sometimes very sombre mood. Even the way he applied his paint was Welsh. He put on paint the way rocks look.

'Then, of course, there were the Kyffin people. Wherever my wife and I travelled round Wales with our children they would always point outside the car and say, Look, there is a Kyffin man! or a Kyffin dog. They are unmistakeably characteristic of Wales.

'And his portraits are wonderful. I was very sad when he ceased to paint them. My brother Tim was director of the National Gallery of Wales. After he died, Kyffin was asked if he would paint his portrait. He had given up portraits but Tim was such a friend he said he would try. He tried to paint from photographs but tore up the result because he said he could not do Tim justice.

'It's not so much the great people he has done as the country people and the children. They are remarkable.'

In 1949, Kyffin painted the portrait of Sir Leonard Twiston-Davies, then director of the National Museum and Gallery of Wales. 'Dad hated it,' his daughter Suzanne recalled. 'He said it made him look like a Welsh mountain. He refused to allow it to be hung and I believe it is still skulking in a cellar at the family home. To compensate Dad, Kyffin gave him a lovely black and white water colour of the Appian Way which he had just painted.'

There were three Kyffin portraits in the Arts Council exhibition that year. The catalogue compiler wrote: 'One feels that portraiture is a professional activity whereas painting the mountains of Gwynedd almost a religion.'

Suzanne added: 'I think, apart from the landscapes, that some of his best pictures are of horses – stout cobs with farmers – both Welsh and Patagonian – trotting along in a purposeful way. Also of Welsh collies, frozen to the ground, stalking the sheep. I have never known a painter who can capture so well the feeling of suspended action, that impression that the dog is about to fly through the air after the flock.

'I also treasure a cartoon he did for me, *Stout Cortez standing on a peke in Darien*. The peke in question was one of my mother's Pekingese.'

Kyffin certainly preferred painting landscapes. He gave up the business of painting portraits with considerable relief. He wrote of the North Wales landscape in an article a few years later: 'An artist can live in North Wales all his life and feel at the end of it he has not completed his work.'

Later, in another magazine, he claimed that the great era of portrait painting was over.

'Portrait painting as a great art has suffered and is now nearly extinct,' he wrote. 'Art historians of the future may say portraiture began in Western Europe with Van Dyck and ended with Kokoschka.

Today the portrait painter tends to use the head as an object to show the agony of our time or to work out clinically an effect of light.'

Kyffin certainly changed that. He would have none of the notion that an artist paints character. He wrote: 'The job of getting a likeness is difficult enough on its own. The painter in the development of the portrait changes the character unintentionally all of the time. A flick of the brush and conceit can be turned into humility, the stroke of a palette knife and strength can be turned to weakness. The character can change maybe three hundred times until finally the artist sees a look in his portrait and says, That is it!'

The Arts Council did not ignore him completely. In a foreword to a booklet it published on Welsh art in 1952 was this praise: 'Kyffin Williams has so made the turbulent mountains of North Wales his subject he might almost be called the Painter of Gwynedd.'

The following year, a painting of Cadair Idris was part of an exhibition organised by what was then the Welsh committee of the Arts Council of Great Britain. In 1956, after a similar exhibition, *The Times* criticised Augustus John's work as flash but said of Kyffin: 'His is one of the two most attractive paintings in the room.'

Indeed, the collection of cuttings from newspapers in the 1950s, held in the archives of Oriel Ynys Mon, is full of praise for his work. The archive also contains a catalogue of a 1957 exhibition in Porthmadog Art Club where Kyffin's works were the cheapest in the show. A buyer could have picked up one of his paintings for £7, and the dearest was £50. A year later at the Tegfryn Art Gallery in Menai Bridge, Anglesey, the price had jumped to £200.

The Tegfryn, which still flourishes, had a strange genesis. Its owner Gwen Brown wanted to raise funds so that the ATC squadron her husband commanded in Menai Bridge could buy a Link trainer. She hit on the idea of a painting sale in her house, and Kyffin was one of the local artists who contributed. The sale was such a success she decided to open a gallery. That gallery, the Tegfryn, became one of the most successful in Wales.

But Kyffin remembered that one of his paintings in that first exhibition was a nude and Mrs Brown was so embarrassed she hid it behind the kitchen door.

It was in her gallery that Mrs Brown encountered the unluckiest art thief in history. She was having coffee with Kyffin when a man walked in with a pile of paintings under his arm. 'Want to buy a painting?' he asked. Mrs Brown saw they were five paintings taken from Kyffin's studio in London. She called Kyffin and the thief shot out, leaving his loot behind. By the time of his next exhibition in 1959 at the Thackeray Gallery in Kensington, a year after the Tegfryn show, the cheapest painting was £325 and the dearest an astronomical (for those days) £575.

One of Kyffin's most successful exhibitions in London came in 1970 when P and D Colnaghi showed his *Drawings from Patagonia*. It was this exhibition, it could be argued, that introduced him to a wider audience. Within four years, he was to become a Royal Academician. Indeed, for many years was the only Welsh RA. By 1997, he had paintings in the collections of the Arts Council of Great Britain; the National Library of Wales; and the National Museum of Wales; the Walker Art Gallery in Liverpool and the Royal Academy. His work was also represented in galleries all over the country, including Swansea, Newport, Hereford and Coventry, and in the collections of many education committees all over Britain.

Typically, Kyffin always maintained that his most successful painting was of a cock pheasant. 'I painted it, shot it, ate it and sold it,' he explained.

Kyffin's Patagonian drawings that were to endear him to a wide audience were the fruit of a Winston Churchill travelling scholarship that he won in 1968.

Only a Welshman can appreciate the call that Patagonia has on the hearts of his countrymen. To an outsider, the story of the trusting farm workers and their families who were persuaded in 1865 to leave their homeland with promises of a golden land in South America, only to find inhospitable desert, is one of cruel exploitation. Welshmen take pride in the way their ancestors irrigated the desert, conquered the hearts of the natives and found prosperity. The sad irony is that in the Falklands War in 1983, Trelew in Patagonia was the biggest base for the Argentinian Air Force that bombed the ship bringing the Welsh Guards to battle. The survivors unknowingly fought Patagonian

Welshmen who had been conscripted into the war. But when Kyffin visited the colony that would be many years into the future.

A thousand miles southwest from Buenos Aires, the Chubut river breaks out from the Andes and carves its way through the sterile plateau of the Patagonian desert to the Atlantic four hundred miles to the east. Forty-four miles from the sea, the river valley widens into a flat land between four and five miles wide. It was here, in a dry, wind-blasted and salt-sodden desert that 150 Welsh men, women and children settled to make a new Wales.

On July 25, 1865, the tea clipper *Mimosa*, from Liverpool, had deposited them on the bleak Patagonian shore in bitter winter storms. Without houses or huts, the settlers carved holes in the cliffs for shelter. Two of the party went ahead with the cattle. Pushing their herd before them, they crossed forty miles of desert before they reached the valley of the Chubut where they made their first settlement.

The Indians, at constant war with Argentina, were ready to massacre the interlopers but they were won over by the gentle ways of the Welsh and their warlike spirits tamed by the soft voices singing in the chapel, one of the first buildings to be erected. Welsh immigrants and Indians became friends, allies in the struggle for existence in those first pioneering years.

The Indians taught the Welsh to hunt the ostrich and the llama. The Welsh taught the Indians to bake bread. Even the Argentine government, delighted that their desert lands were being settled and the Indians pacified, helped with the supply of stock.

At first the crops were poisoned by the deep-lying salt in

the land. Floods washed away their seed and the harsh sun killed the early shoots of corn. The Welsh – fine farmers – criss-crossed the fields with two hundred miles of irrigation canals. Within twenty years the land had been divided into districts, with names like Bethesda, each with its own chapel. The crops were growing and the desert was tamed.

It was then the Indians told their Welsh friends of a beautiful green valley at the foot of the Andes that had no need of irrigation. An advance party of Welsh horsemen trekked across the desert until one of their number saw the valley below them, fresh and green. *'Dyma gwm hyfryd!'* cried one, and Cwm Hyfryd (Delightful Valley) it has been ever since. Two years later, wagon loads of families made the great trek westwards; the towns of Trevelin and Esquel were founded and the success of the Welsh peaceful colonisation was assured. It was a staggering achievement.

Few Welshmen would not wish to visit this South American Wales. For Kyffin it was the dream of a lifetime. He felt the story of the expatriates ought to be recorded in pictures. His enthusiasm persuaded the trustees of the Winston Churchill Memorial Trust to finance a painting trip. Kyffin planned to spend four months in the Welsh province of Chubut, making a record in pictures. Ideally, he would have liked to have spent the time capturing on canvas the people, plants, flowers, birds, animals and landscape, but he realised there was not time for this and decided to let the subjects dictate themselves and to record them as simply and directly as possible.

It was a monumental undertaking. Oils were out of the question. The sheer weight of the paints would be prohibitive in view of the huge areas he planned to cover.

So he bought water colours, designers' colours, coloured inks, pads of paper and a small forest of pencils.

On October 16, 1968, he set sail for South America. From Buenos Aires he flew down to Trelew, the capital of Welsh Patagonia. His arrival in the valley of Chubut was a culture shock. The sense of isolation and the immensity of the place was terrifying. Nothing had prepared him for this narrow valley, sunk below cliffs that called to mind Caerphilly cheese and marked the edge of hundreds of miles of desert. The wind blew continuously, raising dust storms and battering the small oases of willow, poplars and tamarisk the early settlers had planted for protection round their farms.

But the welcome from their descendants was warm. Kyffin found a people so gentle they could not bear to kill the birds that devoured their crops. In consequence, the birds had become tame and took no notice when Kyffin went to draw them. At first he used coloured inks but found them too unsubtle and coarse, so he turned to drawing with a Black Prince pencil, using colour as notes.

The more he worked, the more confident he became. Soon he was using gouache freely to record the wind blasting through the poplars and willows. He found himself reacting to the subject by using the medium it dictated.

The predominant colour was yellow: the desert, the birds, the cactus and the spring flowers. He rejoiced in the flamboyant green and yellow plumage of the *ouraka* that screeched like jays as they raided the orchards. He sketched a thin, shrike-like bird, the *benta-veo*, and flocks of *bandurria*, large birds with grey backs, yellow chests and long, curved red beaks, whose only cry was a mournful 'honk, honk'. In the cliffs parrots nested in their thousands. Handsome birds with blue-green backs and yellow breasts, splashed with red, they swept down on the farms in screeching raids. But the farmers let them be. Indeed, Kyffin's host, Henry Roberts, brought into the house one that had eaten too much to fly. His Welsh forebears would have knocked it on the head. Roberts looked after it until it was fit to fly back to its cliff-top nest. Kyffin was delighted, not only at the humanitarian gesture, but at the opportunity it gave him to draw it in watercolour, catching the subtle relationship between green and blue and yellow plumage.

Drawing so much meant he had many failures but he felt strange when he did not have pencil or fine brush in his hand. He found in Patagonia a love of drawing that stayed with him all his life.

The first settlers had landed at Madryn and Kyffin drew the caves where they had huddled for comfort from the bitter Antarctic gales. He drew the irrigation ditches they had dug and the water wheels on the banks with cans fastened to the paddles. Gradually the despair that had engulfed him when he arrived fell away. He recorded lingering sunsets that moved and twisted blood red and orange in the sky. After a month in Dyffryn Camwy he began to feel a great love for the place. What had been daunting had become beautiful; a beauty of contrast with cliffs brooding over all.

After a month, he moved to the other part of the colony, Cwm Hyfryd, which lies at the foot of the Andes four hundred miles to the west. A mountain man himself, Kyffin looked forward to this as the apogee of the trip. But as he climbed aboard an old Mercedes bus at 5.15 one morning to cross the desert, he was told by his new friends who gathered to see him off at Gaiman that he would soon return.

Dawn came an hour after the rattling bus had left Gaiman, a desert dawn, a cracking, vivid orange that swept across the sky. Soon the dirt road dived towards the Chubut River and the strange rocks that enclosed it.

His destination, Las Plumas, nothing more than an untidy group of houses, was bathed in sunlight when they reached it. Chestnut coloured and cream bellied *guanaco*, Patagonian llamas, more elegant than the coarse Peruvian breed, moved gracefully among sparse shrubs. By now Kyffin was drawing fanatically, making hundreds of small notes in a diary, in the hope that when he reached Esquel and the Andes he could turn them into gouaches. They were crammed with reminders such as 'pink', 'too steep', 'flatter' and 'stratified'.

The bus took him beyond the great cliffs of Los Altares to the Passo des Indios, where the desert began and flocks of ostrich grazed and preened themselves before racing away like fully feathered arrows. Those impressions, too, went down in his diary, fast becoming a disorganised mass of scribbles. Recording, recording, he went further into the desert with its strange outcrops of rock; scribble, scribble, as the sun beat down and then ran before. By the time the bus reached the luscious green valley of Nant y Pysgod, the sun was descending behind the distant Andes and Kyffin's head was throbbing with pain. Continually drawing under the blazing sun produced an agonising migraine. By the time the bus rattled into Esquel he could hardly see.

He was taken in by a kindly Welsh couple. He slept for twelve hours but when he awoke he immediately went back to his 'diaries', as he had come to think of his sketchbooks. In a small shed in the couple's garden he produced the series of gouaches that were to determine the direction his art took. They were like nothing he had ever drawn before, flat, simple and colourful.

Fed and rested, he looked around him at the amazing landscape he saw before him. The mountains above Esquel were topped in red light and in the distance the Cordilleras reared up, pinnacled and snow capped. He was in the land of horsemen, who arrogantly and superbly rode their strong high-stepping horses with one shoulder thrust forward like the Venetian Colleoni statue. Scribble, scribble scribble, they went down in the diaries together with drawings of birds completely different from the flocks in Dyffryn Camwy.

To the south lay Cwm Hyfryd and one day Kyffin climbed into another bus, owned by a South American Dennis Jones, that took him down a road that resembled a ploughed field until another green valley stretched before him: a great bowl of fine agricultural land under the magnificent snow-capped peak of Gorsedd y Cwmyd (Throne in the Clouds).

In Trevelin, in the centre of the valley, Kyffin was welcomed by Senora Gwenonwy Berwyn de Jones to her small house, Ty Ni. When he had moved in, the Senora introduced him to the family of Indians she had adopted. Out came the diaries and the pencil began to fly. He was especially attracted to a tiny girl, Norma, who had huge eyes and made a lovely and delightful model.

The new landscape around him was more like Scotland than Wales. Colours were richer and the area vaster. It was immensely beautiful but it never caught at his heart in the way the lower valleys by the sea had done. In the evenings the sky was a deep blue-black, turning the brown land orange. In Dyffryn Camway the farms had sheltered behind poplars and willows: in the high mountains whirling clouds burst through peaks and sudden cyclones shivered the windows in the houses. It was not watercolour land. Gouache was the medium for the rich, rugged valley.

Kyffin was loaned a piebald horse as transport. It seemed a good idea and a convenient way to tour the valley, but he soon discovered drawing from the saddle was difficult and the view from ground level differed in subtle ways from the higher prospect of the saddle.

Yet it was the horse that took him to the greatest triumph of his trip. He rode to a farm called Fron Deg where he met a patriarch, a tall, spare 88-year-old called Brychan Evans with a distinguished head and the springy bow legs of the horseman. In Evans's parlour Kyffin tried to record his proud head as the patriarch sat looking out of the window at the distant mountains that had been his life. The drawing would not work. Kyffin was incapable of doing the grand old man justice. Part in temper and part depressed, he returned to his room at Ty Ni. For hours he wrestled with that wonderful face until at last he produced a watercolour portrait that satisfied him. It was not only like Evans: it was the head of all the Patagonian Welshmen who had won a living against terrific odds. Kyffin felt that portrait alone justified his four months of almost continuous painting and drawing.

Years later he was to write: 'My visit to the Welsh in Patagonia was of the utmost value to my art. I was there for a purpose which drove me to draw with an intensity that had never been possible before. To make such a record as I did in Patagonia is a great incentive. It imposes discipline, essential to a writer or a musician but often forgotten by painters.'

Ever after, Patagonia held a special place in his heart. When in 1991 he published the second volume of biographical notes, *A Wider Sky*, the account of his Patagonian adventure was a high spot. He wrote in that book: 'They didn't know what to make of me. My Welsh was catastrophic. They said I didn't speak Welsh but for me it was the most exciting and memorable period of my life.'

Chapter nine

In 1970 when Kyffin was elected a Royal Academician, he decided to give up teaching and return to Wales. Four years later, an increasingly popular painter with the art buying public, he came home to Anglesey with an assured income.

He said: 'I could not stay in London. I was becoming schizophrenic in my painting. In Wales I looked at the mountains and felt wonderful. I knew exactly what I wanted to paint. When I got back to London, like most Welshmen I became possessed by a fatal Cymric nostalgia which blotted out what I wanted to say in my pictures.'

People who love Anglesey have difficulty in persuading outsiders of its special quality. Mainlanders claim that its main function is as a platform from which to view the beauties of Snowdonia. Those fortunate enough to live there know that at the beguiling heart of its appeal is a sense of ancient place. Anglesey was the last stronghold of the Druids in Europe. The names of its fields – The Field of the Long Battle, the Field of Bitter Lamentation in the parish of Brynsiencyn – recall the Roman invasion. A house called 'Shout', on an eminence from which tribesmen could see the Strait, recalls warnings of Norsemen invaders.

When RAF Valley was under construction during the early part of World War II, the runway was made of packed sand. In order to bind it, workmen brought tons of mud from Llyn Cerrig Bach, which in the Dark Age of the Princes had been a lake. A tractor stuck in the mud and when it was hauled out, it had a chain attached to it which proved to be a Celtic slave chain. Fortunately, the driver had the presence of mind not to throw it away. Later, excavations led to the discovery of a hoard of weapons and chariot harness. It is believed they were thrown in the lake by Druids seeking to placate an ancient war god. Perhaps the story of Excalibur is a folk memory of that tradition.

Kyffin had never lost touch with the island home of his ancestors. His cousin Betty Mewies knew how important the island was to him: 'Kyffin always said what he thought. I think the reason was that he was so secure and the reason for that is Anglesey. He felt so right there. He was part of it and it gave him a security which allowed him to say what he liked. Our family tree goes back to the eleventh century. All on Anglesey.'

Wendy Davies had more memories of Kyffin's early life: 'My great Aunt Cecily Vivian had the Anglesey Beagles after the war and Kyffin and I hunted a lot with them. Great Aunt Cecily played a big part in his life. She was a really sparky old lady. She was a very positive woman. If he was in one of his dumps, you would hear her say: If you are in the dumps you can turn round and go home. She gave him a lot of support. Although she had this tough exterior she had a great appreciation of art.

'But she was certainly tough. On one occasion she went hunting in Ireland with her husband. At one hunt, Uncle Cyril came off. Someone came up to Aunt Cecily and said: Your husband has fallen off. As she galloped after the hounds, Aunt Cecily called over her shoulder: Send him to the kennels.

'My grandfather was very scornful of Anglesey families. 'All they do is chase girls, empty bottles and litigate,' he would say.'

Kyffin had a much higher opinion of the island's leading families. There was just a suggestion of benevolent snob about the way he cherished them. Certainly he knew their histories and could be wildly indiscreet. At one dinner table he enlarged on his belief that no leading Anglesey family was what it seemed.

'There is no family as old as mine in the direct line,' he told the assembled company. 'The Bulkeleys are really Williamses, the Pagets are really Baileys and the Lloyds are Jones Parrys. The reason is evident. People changed their names to inherit land. Anglesey is an odd place.

'In the 18th century it was ruled by its squires. They were a benevolent group and, on the rise of non-conformism, the squires made generous gifts of land to the chapels. Little did they realise they were building Trojan horses. The chapels bred resentment of the squirearchy. By the beginning of the 19th century, power had been transferred to the chapels and the squires had nothing left but their pedigrees. So they retreated to their houses, only communicating with other land owners and comparing the length of their family trees. They became the most monumental snobs. They were known as The Toffee Noses of North Wales and their families are riven with feuds. Before there were bridges, feuding and cohabiting was all they did.

'I remember a terrible feud about the sacking of a huntsman of the Anglesey Hounds. My great uncle Tom Rice Roberts was master and he appointed a man called Davies as huntsman who was always drunk. That was no problem. Everyone drank because there was nothing else to do. When the mastership was taken over by Evelyn Meyrick, who sacked Davies, Anglesey was riven.

'There was a GP in Llangefni, Dr Llywelyn Jones. He was terribly keen on getting in with the Anglesey gentry so he went out hunting, beautifully turned out. Top hat, green coat and a nice horse. Fine figure of a man and very popular with the wives of members. His progeny, under other names, are in the island now. There are some people on the island who are related to me but they do not know it and would be horrified if they did. Hanky panky was known in Anglesey as having a gallop.'

Kyffin's knowledge of Anglesey pedigrees was encyclopaedic:

A man called Williams left the Vaynol estate across the Straits from us to George II. The king didn't want it, so he gave it in turn to a minor court functionary called Smith. Smith then added Assheton to his name. What the king did not know was that the land included much of Snowdonia and also the quarries which were to bring the Assheton Smiths an enormous fortune. An Assheton Smith heiress married a Robin Duff, who became Duff Assheton Smith. His son, Michael Duff, married the Marquess of Anglesey's elder sister Caroline, one of the great beauties of the day. His sister married a Lord Glenconner, who was a Tennant. When Michael Duff died, the money went to the Tennants.

Michael Duff and Caroline had an adopted child, Charlie, but he did not inherit. Caroline was the painter Rex Whistler's great love and a great friend of Tallulah Bankhead. She would have married Rex but he was killed in the war when he got out of his tank under heavy fire to free it from wire.

The Queen Mother was a frequent visitor to Vaynol

and Tony Armstrong Jones was a godson. I knew his great aunt. His uncle, a man called Howden Armstrong Jones, lived in Eisteddfa, a house near ours on the Llyn, near Criccieth. He wore loud checks and put on a Welsh accent. My father hated him but his sister Ginny Armstrong Jones was lovely. She called me her little platinum. Armstrong Jones was always pestering Lloyd George for a knighthood. In the end he got one, by mistake. It should have gone to another Armstrong Jones from Liverpool.

Perhaps the two people Kyffin most dearly loved were the Marquess and Marchioness of Anglesey. He dedicated *A Wider Sky* to the Marchioness and in it told how she and the Marquess had found him a home on their estate, a converted inn at Pwllfanogl, where he lived until his death.

He described it to a friend:

> I live and work on the edge of an old harbour. The waters of the Menai Strait wash almost to my front door and the River Braint flows through the woods behind the house, under a bridge and through the harbour to the Strait a hundred yards from my front door.
>
> There could be no better place for an artist to live. Across the Strait I can see the mountains, the Carneddau, Elidir Fawr, Snowdon and the hills that edge down to Pen Llyn. The great bow of the Strait bends westwards to Caernarfon and the open sea. To the east it winds through the Swellie rocks, under the bridges, to the Great Orme at Llandudno. Fishermen launch their boats at the front of my house and the Bangor trawlers make for Porth Penrhyn with accompanying seagulls crowding in their wake. On summer evenings terns dive for fish.
>
> On the longest day of the year the sun rises over the

island above the spire of Llanfairpwllgwyngyll church and for six months I watch it rising until on December 22 it appears over the western slopes of Elidir. Throughout the year it creates a footpath of light across the water to my house. I make colour notes and later try to turn them into paintings in my studio in the garden.

Painting the sea is a battle like the one the sea fights with the land. I aim to keep the picture fluid and the paint rich and sensuous. But it is so difficult to get the light to rest on the sea in the right perspective and so easy to lose it by some ill-judged movement of the brush.'

In *A Wider Sky* Kyffin told of a small boy who visited him at Pwllfanogl: 'As we stood at the water's edge with gentle waves breaking at our feet the little boy looked up at me. What will happen to you here when you die? he asked with a look of concern on his face. I knew I had to answer with a confidence I did not possess. Oh it will be wonderful, I said. I shall slip into the sea and be swept away by the water and I shall be carried under the bridges and away to Penmon and the open sea. Oh yes it will be rather wonderful...'

Kyffin's circle of friends embraced not only the leading families. He loved the country people and drew and painted them endlessly. In the views of many, those portraits and prints were among the greatest of his works and the ones that will live in memory the longest.

No artist ever got nearer to the hearts of people who would never dream of setting foot in an art gallery. He took them as his subjects. Children who sat for him in his early days got half a crown, a cup of tea and a slice of his mother's delicious Swiss roll.

The portrait of one early sitter, Gwilym Islwyn Owen, won Kyffin the Slade Portrait Award. Years later, in 1989, they met again when Owen was working as a car park attendant in Criccieth. 'Some weeks later,' Owen recalled, 'a lady drove up with a parcel for me. It was the painting and it came with a note from Kyffin remembering when it was painted. I will treasure it all my life.'

Kyffin could be critical. Shortly after he moved to Pwllfanogl and before care for the environment became a fashionable issue, he told Arthur Williams, the *Daily Post* columnist, of his worries that the Menai Strait was becoming polluted.

He said: 'Welsh people are apathetic about their surroundings. Basically, it is the English who are most concerned by the ruination of the landscape. The Welsh are terribly concerned about the language but they don't use their eyes. I find this very extraordinary. If the Welsh Language Society put the same energy into the conservation of the Welsh landscape that they do into the conservation of the language it would be a great benefit to the nation.'

In his early days painting portraits he had sacrificed accuracy of tone by using a dark line to draw into the thick paint, defining each area one from another. As his confidence grew, he dispensed with the line and painted only tonally and always with a knife. He used few colours because he believed that extra colour complicated the portrait, and the fewer the colours, the more accurate the tone must be. His best results were achieved, he thought, with only black, white, cadmium red and yellow ochre.

His most difficult subjects were girls and young women

and he reckoned it took him twenty years to learn how to paint them. He was happier painting farmers, labourers, people in homes for the blind and the old.

The blind fascinated him. He wondered at their peaceful resignation, their wet lips always moving and the eternity of space in their dead eyes. He always painted against a flat, bright background and when the painting was dry he would take it back to the blind subject so that they could pass fingers over the ridge of paint, feeling ears, eyes and hair.

He described painting 92-year-old Mrs Stanley of Beaumaris as she sat in a huge green armchair, dressed in an ultramarine frock, her tiny head covered in lace-like hair, her face soft and pink and her long hands moving continually.

'As I painted, she hummed strange hymn tunes. Occasionally she would break off to utter disconcerting remarks about God's determination to take her as he had taken the rest of her friends. You know not the day nor the hour, she warned me. Then she fell asleep and I finished the painting to the sound of her snores, mixed with the cry of the seagulls and the noise of cars in the street below.'

Other sittings were less tranquil. An Anglesey farmer sat on an oak settle. The flickering flames from the kitchen fire danced on his cheeks making it difficult to find the right tone and colour. At last Kyffin gave up and the farmer came over to see what he had done. 'Well, well, well,' he said in his slow Anglesey voice, 'everything is going wrong. My motor is broke down, my tractor's big end is gone, my milling machine won't work, and now you can't paint my face.'

Anglesey farmers have mixed views about artists. At Benllech, Kyffin's car became stuck in wet sand and a farmer used a chain and a Fergie tractor to haul him out. In gratitude, Kyffin, who had no money, tore the painting he had just completed off his sketching block and gave it to the farmer. Then watched in horror as the farmer folded the painting into quarters and stuffed it in his overall pocket.

Anglesey folk take a gritty view of life. When he decided to live in Pwllfanogl he went to see an old lady, Maggie Williams, Penymynydd, who used to help his mother in the house. A huge, raw boned woman, humorous and very earthy, she told him if he was going to Pwllfanogl he would have to find a woman. Kyffin jibbed: 'What if we don't get on?' and she said, 'If you don't get on, *Duw*, it's a grand place to drown the bugger.'

When he came home after being discharged from the army, Kyffin was looked after by an old family nurse Sarah Richards. One day she said she had a treat for him. 'I am going to take you to where my brother Bob lives. I will introduce you to his housekeeper Miss Hughes. She has three daughters and neither one of them is sisters.'

About to begin painting in Cwm Bychan, he got out of his car to feel a presence behind him. He turned to see a short, stocky aboriginal Welsh woman who rapped out in Welsh, 'Ten pence.' He told her that he was Welsh. 'Where do you come from?' she asked. He told her, 'Ynys Mon.'

'That will be twenty pence,' she replied.

Kyffin's cultural contribution to Wales has been immense

and is now widely recognised. Less well known is the work he did silently for charity.

Dr Jim Davies OBE, and his wife Nesta worked tirelessly for charities in North Wales and between them raised millions of pounds. They said people had no idea how many pictures and prints Kyffin had given to help others.

'He was very kind to me when I was working with muscular dystrophy,' said Nesta, 'but he was generous to so many causes it would be impossible to list them. He painted austere mountains and was like a rock himself. He was as deep as the sea but also full of humour.'

Dr Jim was one of Wales's doughtiest fighters. During the war he was a special services wireless operator who flew on bomber raids in an aircraft that went in before the bombers to jam the German equipment. It was incredibly dangerous. Of the seven sergeants who joined his squadron, two were killed and he was shot down on his second mission. For six months he lived with the Dutch resistance, until a double agent betrayed him to the Gestapo. He was sent to a series of POW camps before being force-marched hundreds of miles from Stalag Luft 7 in Poland to Berlin.

After the war, he became principal of Bangor Normal College of Higher Education. When senior civil servants in the Ministry of Education decided to close it as part of a rationalisation policy, Dr Jim organised the campaign to keep it open and led an all-party deputation to the Secretary of State for Education Fred Mulley. Mulley said he would give them five minutes but they were with him for two hours. Subsequently, he decided to reverse the decision to close the college. It was the only time he rejected the advice of his top civil servants. The college now lives on as part of the University of Wales. How did Dr Jim persuade the minister?

'Lord Cledwyn tipped me off that Fred Mulley had also been a prisoner of war and advised me to mention my POW days. So, talking about the Butler 1944 education act, I said at that time we were both guests of the Führer.'

Jim recalled the campaign he ran to raise funds for a scanner at Ysbyty Gwynedd: 'We were determined the new building would be friendly, artistic and exciting. So you may imagine how delighted we were when Kyffin gave us prints for every wall and promised to do the same for new haematology and cancer units.'

He also explained why painters have so many hurdles to leap to gain acceptance in Wales. 'Painting and the visual arts are not part of the Welsh cultural background,' he said. 'We were brought up on literature and music, the Eisteddfod culture. We do not take painting seriously enough. When I spoke at the opening of the Royal Cambrian Academy Summer Exhibition in 1998, I supported Kyffin's view that it was a disgrace that in the magnificent National Art Gallery and Museum in Cardiff there was not a single room devoted to Welsh art. The first curator had said such a room would diminish our European contribution. Rubbish, said Kyffin, and I agreed with him. Cardiff is a significant capital and I am delighted that in the end Kyffin was listened to and, thanks to him, our national art has a fitting home there.

'Historically, there were no patrons here. In Europe, you had the church: in England, powerful aristocrats. In Wales you had only the things that were free: the voice and the word. And the non-conformist tradition took no account of the visual arts. The economy in Wales was based on pastoral farming, which meant there was no money for painting and sculpture. Wales had to express itself in the cheapest way possible.'

Kyffin fought ceaselessly for a place in the Welsh sun for the country's painters. He was twice president of the Royal Cambrian Academy, persuading some of the finest artists in Wales to exhibit at its superb modern gallery in Conwy.

Vicky MacDonald was director of the RCA during those years. She remembered: 'He was a superb chairman and because of his stature commanded respect all over the art world. His first stint as president ended acrimoniously in 1976 when our headquarters were in an Elizabethan mansion in the town, Plas Mawr. It was owned by Lord Mostyn, who told us that the house was in very bad condition and needed half a million pounds spending on it.

'He agreed the Cambrian had a 99-year lease and could not be moved but urged us to move anyway. At Kyffin's suggestion, he offered us what is now the Mostyn, a purpose built gallery in Llandudno, at a very reasonable rent. However, the members did not want to move and Kyffin resigned in despair.'

Over the years standards fell at the Cambrian until it became little more than a sketching club. But happier days were ahead. A new president, Jack Shore, and his committee organised a brilliantly successful fund-raising campaign, which resulted in the Academy acquiring a new purpose-built gallery adjacent to their old home, Plas Mawr. Kyffin agreed to come back as president.

Said Vicky: 'He immediately took responsibility for raising the standards and included Article 15 in the charter, whereby artists of quality could be invited to become members without having to pass scrutiny by Academy members. He was the ideal president. He was always ready to help in any way he could, rarely missed a meeting unless he was ill, and bubbled with new ideas. He knew everyone in the art world and certainly knew how the art world works.'

It was a casual meeting on a railway station that launched Kyffin on a new career as an author. Anna Haycraft was waiting on a platform at Euston for a train home to Penmaenmawr. She had been working at a Cheshire Home but was disillusioned with Captain Leonard Cheshire, whose ideas on hygiene she found bizarre. She decided to leave and enter a convent.

Kyffin recalled seeing this very attractive girl and introducing himself. 'We talked all the way to Penmaenmawr where her mother lived,' he said. 'She told me she was going into a convent and I thought, what a terrible waste. She did go into the convent but she slipped a disc, had to go to hospital and never went back. She married the publisher Colin Haycraft and they had seven children. I fell in love with her the first time we met.'

Anna, who as Alice Thomas Ellis became a best-selling novelist, remembered their brief encounter: 'It was forty years ago and I was an art student. There was this man and we got into conversation. I thought he was absolutely fascinating. I didn't see him for a few years and then we met by chance. Freddy Uhlman was a mutual friend, Colin and I went to his house and there was this delightful person I had met on the train. I had never forgotten him but I believed I would never see him again. We have been friends ever since.

'I didn't know he was in love with me. I love Kyffin, I

always have. He was very important in my life because he was one of the very few good people that I have known and he was funny with it. He was the best company you could ever have. He was witty and wise and funny. I thought he was wary of marriage because of the epilepsy. In any case, I loved him far too much to marry him. I think he was almost too good to marry. I don't know any woman who could have matched up to him. He was so dedicated to his art, I think a woman would have felt she took second place. I recognised in Kyffin a quality so unusual I do not think it has a name. Purity, perhaps. People you marry, you tend to fight with, and I could not imagine ever fighting with him.

'I cannot imagine Kyffin married. His attraction for women? I can't speak for other women. I just found him incredibly lovable, and not only lovable, intensely likeable. You never felt threatened by him. He is a very difficult man to encapsulate.

'My children absolutely doted on him. They called him Uncle Kyffin. He was what I expected an uncle to be – and a gentleman, too, if it comes to that.

'As an artist I think he was, and is, supreme. Wales is grey and green, black and white, and I think he latched on to that. I don't think watercolours work here and I am sure he is the only painter who has got Wales as it is. I have wondered whether the epilepsy had anything to do with his talent. Interesting how he could stand in a howling gale and not feel cold at all until he stopped painting.'

It was a phenomenon that puzzled Kyffin too. 'It is very odd. I can stand in the snow for hours with the temperature below freezing point and yet my hands remain warm until I stop painting,' he told me. 'My left hand, which holds the palette, even though motionless in the frosty air, remains comfortably warm. Only when I pack up do I feel cold. I imagine that unconsciously I practise yoga.'

Anna had another explanation: 'Painting was for Kyffin what religion is to me. He creates the world that is and adds something to it. Incidentally, he was wrong about one thing. He said I left the convent. I did not. The convent slung me out because of the slipped disc. If you are a postulant and you cannot work you are no good. I am going back when I get the chance.'

Kyffin's first book *Across the Straits* was published by Anna's husband Colin, who ran the publishers Duckworth & Co. He dedicated it to Anna. The book, which came out in 1973, caused a storm among the *uchelwyr* of Gwynedd who considered that he told too many of their secrets.

Lord Crickhowell revealed that after the success of *Across the Straits,* Kyffin wrote a sequel by hand and sent it – the only copy – to Duckworth's. 'He wrote it not long after *Across the Straits.* Haycraft insisted it was sent off to a reader, despite the success of the first book. Unfortunately, the reader, who was a considerable pornographer, got word he might be raided by the police, so he burned all his pornographic books. Alas, he included – not I think on grounds of pornography – the only text of *A Wider Sky,* which was, as I say, hand-written. Poor Kyffin was deeply upset and it took him a long time before he could bring himself to write it again. Not surprisingly, it is not as vigorous as *Across the Straits.'*

Chapter ten

By 1969, Kyffin had put on thirty one-man exhibitions but the golden years began in 1970 when he was elected Associate of the Royal Academy. From then until his death honours gathered like swallows on a wire. In 1974 he became a full Royal Academician; in 1978 an honorary MA of the University of Wales; in 1983 he received an OBE; in 1987 he was appointed a deputy lieutenant of Gwynedd; in 1989 a deputy fellow of the University of Wales, Swansea; in 1991 an honorary fellow of the University of Wales, Bangor; and in the same year won the Medal of the Honourable Society of Cymrodorion. In 1992 it was the turn of the University College of Wales, Aberystwyth, to make him an honorary fellow. In the same year, he became president of the Royal Cambrian Academy for the second time, a member of the arts advisory committee of the National Museum of Wales and a member of the court of governors of the National Library of Wales. In the following year, 1993, the University of Wales celebrated its centenary by making him an honorary doctor of letters, in company with the Aga Khan and Mary Robinson, the President of Eire. The degrees were presented by the Prince of Wales.

In 1993 also, Prifysgol Cymru (University of Wales) made him an honorary DLitt in recognition of his own six books, *Across the Straits; A Wider Sky; Portraits; Land and Sea;* a Gregynog limited edition of his Mabinogion illustrations; and a book of cartoons, *Boyo Ballads*. He also illustrated five books for other authors, including *A Welsh Anthology* by

Alice Thomas Ellis; *The Astonishing Infantry: the History of the Royal Welsh Fusiliers* by Michael Glover; *Patagonia Revisited* by Bruce Chatwin and Paul Theroux; and *Two Old Men* by Kate Roberts.

By 1970, he had put on four exhibitions at Colnaghi's in London; six at the Leicester Galleries, London; one at the Glynn Vivian Art Gallery in Swansea; another at the Howard Roberts Gallery in Cardiff; and five at the Tegfryn Gallery in Menai Bridge. In addition, he had staged four retrospective exhibitions. From 1975, he had biennial exhibitions at the Thackeray Gallery in London and the Albany Gallery, Cardiff. He was issuing limited editions of greatly sought after prints, painting two pictures a week and living a very full social life until his final illness.

His greatest moment came with the New Year honours in 1999 when he was awarded a knighthood in recognition of his services to the visual arts. He was delighted. He felt that his war with the establishment had been vindicated by the establishment itself. He was very happy, too, that the first letter of congratulations came from the Prince of Wales. He held the Prince in high esteem and the feeling was obviously reciprocated.

His army of friends was delighted though some were apprehensive that he might not turn up for the investiture. They recalled his 80th birthday celebrations, when the various organisations to which he contributed so much sought to honour him with presentations. Wales Tourist Board, for example, arranged a reception at the Royal Academy, with a show of his Patagonian paintings, to which the Argentinian ambassador was invited. Kyffin pleaded illness and said he could not attend. Other presentations shared the same fate. An exception was an

Arts Fund luncheon, where he made a brief appearance at the end of the lunch, but only because it was at Plas Newydd, the home of his great friends the Marquess and Marchioness of Anglesey.

Before receiving his knighthood, he had been created an OBE. He hired a morning coat to attend the investiture. But even then there was a contretemps. Walking across to the Palace, he felt a stabbing pain in his foot. When he examined the shoe he found there was a hole in it. Looking round for something to cover it, all he could find was an empty cheese-flavoured crisps packet. Folding it, he slipped it into the shoe. It was comfortable enough, but as he waited for his turn to be invested, his nostrils were assailed by the smell of cheese. The warmth of the room had released the aroma from the packet. Urgently, he asked a passing courtier if he had some spare paper. The courtier obliged, then watched with amazement as Kyffin took off his shoe, removed the crisps packet and replaced it with the paper. 'Thank you, that is much better,' he told the courtier.

In 1998, the Prince of Wales invited him to Highgrove to see his watercolours. Clearly too shy to discuss them, he did not meet Kyffin again after he had seen them. The Prince need not have worried. Kyffin was very impressed. 'Some were very good indeed,' he said.

There were increasing signs that the establishment was taking him to its bosom. A fortnight after the knighthood, the Welsh Secretary Alun Michael 'dropped in' on Kyffin at Pwllfanogl. He told a reporter, who just happened to be there, what a huge fan he was of Kyffin; he had brought with him a treasured copy of Kyffin's Landscapes of Wales.

'I think most people would be jealous of my having the

opportunity to meet Kyffin,' he said. 'You don't often have the chance to say thank you to somebody who has given so much pleasure. I think he reflects the sort of confidence and pride we need in things that are Welsh. I was delighted to hear of his knighthood. It reflected something which many people throughout Wales wanted to say. His paintings have captured something that is very important, combining art with the mood of the countryside, the mountains, the weather and the sea.'

Mr Michael confided that one of Kyffin's lino-cuts hung on the wall of his House of Commons office and there were two of his paintings in the Welsh Office. It was a graceful tribute but cynical observers noted that Mr Michael was in the middle of an election battle with Rhodri Morgan for the leadership of the Welsh Assembly.

Not all members of the royal family were Kyffin fans. A large and very fine painting he had presented to the Princess Royal mysteriously surfaced some years later at an Anglesey auction house.

Kyffin pretended not to be impressed with the knighthood. As with everything that happened to him, he turned it into an anecdote to amuse his friends: 'When Downing Street rang to ask me if I would accept one, I thought they were joking. Odd business. When the letter came, it had two boxes, and you had to tick a 'yes' box if you wanted a knighthood and a 'no' box if you didn't.'

His friend Lord Crickhowell is a perceptive critic of Kyffin's work. 'There was a period when his painting was very dark,' he said. 'We always used to say, Kyffin, can't you brighten up? But he could not. Then suddenly, as he got older, he seemed to break out of this dark period and started painting seascapes with great flaring suns, all scarlets and yellows. At his 1998 Albany exhibition there were some tremendous snowscapes. Painting of a kind that twenty years ago you would never have seen.

'His cartoons were another development. He gave me a very amusing cartoon about my trouble with the plan for a Cardiff Opera House. It shows an opera singer and a rugby player. On another occasion he was helping my daughter Olivia to paint and there was paint all over the kitchen. My wife told them both off and that produced another cartoon.

'He remained very much the Painter of Gwynedd, as he was described at the beginning of his career. It's interesting that though he often stayed with us in the Black Mountains, he could not paint there. He was most at home in North Wales. He could paint in Pembrokeshire because of the sea but he seemed unable to catch the gentle softness of the Black Mountains; perhaps even the light. Light was very important to him. I always thought it had something to do with his epilepsy. Clearly it affected the way he painted. Epileptics are profoundly affected by light. My wife, who had a mild epileptic condition, hates sitting under strobe lamps. They have an immediate effect on her.

'Whatever the reason, he didn't paint here, alas. It is that tremendous sense of drama – and light and dark – of North Wales that he couldn't find in Breconshire. I have one drawing. It's about the only one he has ever done in all the years he stayed here with us, or before that at my father's cottage across the bridge.'

Crickhowell's father, Ralph Edwards, discussing Kyffin's drawings in 1964, drew attention to Kyffin's

174

devotion to his own land:

> Kyffin Williams is among the most gifted contemporary painters for whom nature has continued to suffice. He is a Welsh artist in the romantic tradition (as were J D Innes and Augustus John) and his art is deeply imbued with the Celtic spirit; which is recognisable too in the work of his elder contemporaries – in the visionary world of David Jones and in Ceri Richards's colour and rhythms.
>
> He has a deep feeling for a type of scenery with which he has been familiar since childhood and an intuitive understanding of its essential characteristics, which an alien can scarcely obtain.
>
> His drawings are those of a painter. Many are in fact studies for paintings, all done on the spot. His oils and his drawings are unmistakably by the same hand. In the drawings, broad washes are often put on with a full brush and the thick contour lines are sharply defined.
>
> When colour is used at all in his preparatory studies it is used sparingly in a scale of muted hues; volumes, forms, atmosphere. Distances are rendered largely by strong contrasts of tone, the white of the paper being often foiled against black. Thus resonant effects of light and dark are obtained with plastic illusion, ink wash being the medium most often employed. But this is no facile formula or convention; the drawings are interpretative, expressing a highly personal vision – the spirit in preference to the physical facts. It is not gentle or elegiac nor does it breathe the *douce mélancholie de la campagne*; the landscape of the artist's predilection is far from sweet; much of it is melancholy, sombre or austere...
> ...his vigorous, expressive style, which has no close parallel and is identifiable at a glance, is admirably adapted to record his subjective impressions of nature...'

Professor David Carpanini, RA, held the chair of Fine Art at the University of Wolverhampton and is president of the Royal Society of Painters and Printmakers. He met Kyffin when they were both elected to the Academy in 1974. He said, quite simply: 'To call Kyffin a friend has been an honour and a privilege and I am one of many who has been inspired by his enormous knowledge of art, his generosity of spirit and his artistic integrity.

'I was always impressed by his extraordinary generosity to young artists once he sensed they were making an effort to work towards their vision. He must have been a charismatic teacher at Highgate. Although he always made light of his time there I remember when we had a house at Llanberis he brought round a portfolio of the boys' work. My wife Janet and I were struck by the way he knew exactly what had happened to all of them. Of course he had distinguished pupils like Patrick Proctor and Anthony Green but there were others who did not go into the world of art.

'What was impressive about the portfolio was that there was no evidence of a house style. No one had tried to imitate Kyffin. They were trying to follow their own visions. That is the mark of a good teacher.

'I find it extraordinary that he did not get wide recognition from the UK establishment and from those self-appointed arbiters of taste with their prejudices and fashions who could not see in him what he truly was, a major contemporary painter. He consistently followed a strong personal vision with total truth and I think that is what the public recognise, perhaps without knowing it, and why they appreciate him so much.

'He never found painting or drawing easy. But he loved

his subject and struggled to find a consistent quality of newness. He was never a repeatist artist. There was a variety in the way he handled his subject which was mesmeric. His paintings work on two levels. They have a strong narrative and at the same time an aesthetic appeal. Great art must work on those levels and that is the reason I believe his work will live long after most of his more fashionable contemporaries are forgotten.

'It is a measure of his painting that you do not have to look for clever words to respond to it. The way he applies paint to a canvas could be deterrent but it is not. There is an abstract quality which is very engaging. He articulates his vision so precisely and his method of doing so is at one with his spiritual dimension. The public sense that his pictures are right. Here is honesty and truth. They have all stood on a headland and felt the sea spray in their face. Here it is on canvas.

'Anyone who goes to art with an open mind and heart is rewarded. It is only the person who brings their baggage of prejudice who cannot see its quality.'

It was difficult to get Kyffin to talk of his methods, though much was written about him and he was filmed many times. At the time Ralph Edwards was writing his critique quoted above, Kyffin spoke in an interview about his style. Thirty years later he agreed it had altered little.

> First I lay in the outlines of my subject with a brush. Then also with a brush I cover the whole area with a tone darker than my final painting. I do this because I can let the dark through here and there as I want, to give points of vitality and strength to the picture. I use very little white at this stage to avoid chalkiness.

The palette I use in the studio is flake white, ivory black, Windsor yellow, yellow ochre, burnt umber, cobalt blue and cobalt green. Outdoors I add vermilion and French ultramarine. You must have vermilion for bracken. I use flake white in preference to titanium or zinc white because they have no weight for my knife.

When I paint mountains I know what is on the other side. For eighteen months at the Slade I floundered hopelessly. All the other students seemed so brilliant. Their line drawing was uncanny and their general air of artistic awareness was frightening.

One day Professor Schwabe was giving me a lesson in line drawing. Williams, Williams, he said, why do you make your nudes look like oak trees? He advised me to paint but at first I could find neither impulse nor enthusiasm to pull me along and make up for my lack of facility.

And then one day in the Ashmolean I saw a reproduction of Piero della Francesca's *Resurrection*. I realised then how much really did come from things, from people, from the hills and mountains; from rivers and waterfalls and the sea and how much I wanted to paint them.

So I started to paint seriously. I worked fast since I was so desperate to see my pictures finished and alive in front of me. The great library of my boyhood experiences came back to me as if I had filed them away for this purpose. I was 24 and had been an art student for eighteen months. I was beginning to find myself and all the energy that had made me pursue unfortunate foxes, dream of cavalry charges, winning the Grand National or scoring a winning try for Wales was put into painting the things I began to realise I loved dearly.

From that moment there was no search for technique. My intense interest was to put down what I saw or what was in my mind. The subject dictated how it was done. I found myself painting in a manner that surprised me, and one in which I had never seen a picture painted before. They may have been poor things but at least they were my own.

I began to realise how lucky I was to have been brought up in the countryside. The scudding light on a hillside suddenly became more exciting, more electric; the heavy cloud over Snowdon more moving. I found myself walking miles over the mountains, making hundreds of drawings, carrying paints and canvasses up onto windy ridges and down the scree, seeking out the places I had known so well in the past.

Shortly before his death, Kyffin looked back over the years between that eager young man and the time when he was widely acknowledged as Wales's greatest living painter.

People assume that painting is a pleasure. I don't enjoy painting, there is the pressure and the duty. You cannot afford to luxuriate. You have to put it on canvas. And there are seasons like spring and autumn when painting is very difficult indeed. In spring you get the mountains still dressed for winter: cold, blue-grey. Against them, you get the lemon of a sycamore in the valleys. I only once managed to paint that well. It was a picture called *Lleder Valley in Spring*.

It bothered me until I realised that none of the great artists had ever painted spring or autumn successfully. Turner did vaguely but Constable didn't. It never works over grass because green and brown just don't go together and green, anyway, is just so difficult. I now mute a rich green and in some ways that is a lie. But it is the only way colours work.

It was important to Kyffin to relate to the people, which is why his paintings cost so little in comparison to the price lesser painters charged. He explained: 'In the past Welsh ministers, miners and farmers could not buy paintings. Now, thanks to improved education, their sons have entered the professions and have a larger disposable income, but it's still not too large. Coming from the same roots as they do, I painted the places they wanted to be reminded of.

'I am the first Welsh painter who has been able to live and work in Wales. I may also be the first artist to get through to the Welsh public but I have never appealed to the art establishment. Being the only Welsh born RA was unfortunate because they resented it. There is something in the Welsh character that is displeased by success in England. Welsh people were often nominated but they attracted very few votes.

'I am glad the Welsh people like my work and call me Kyffin. My development has been very gradual because I never considered myself a serious painter until the sixties. Before that, I thought I was painting for the good of my health. I never kept a record of the paintings I sold. I did not have any ambition to be a proper painter. I wanted to teach in an art school but no art school would have me because it was the time when they were jettisoning the idea of drawing. However incapable I might have been at the Slade, if you are obsessed, as I luckily have been, obsession can create talent. I am not a natural draughtsman but I was so obsessed with recording Wales and its people it forced me to learn how to draw. I have never wanted to change my style, just to paint better and there was a lot of room for that.

'I started selling well when I moved from Bond Street to Kensington in 1974. I have had twelve exhibitions there (one every other year) and each year I have sold better. Partly because my pictures are cheap. Most artists charge too much and then complain that they don't sell. If they worked harder and sold for less they would sell far more. But artists think they are great and have to put whacking great prices on their work. I do not know why people like my work. I don't particularly. There are none of my paintings in my house. Couldn't bear to have them.

'I had wonderful preparation for the life of an artist. The worst thing is to be eulogised when you are young. With me, it has been a gradual climb and just right. I have never actually considered I am a success. If I did it would be the end. If any artist ever thinks he has arrived he has had it.

'I have had a very odd life. Very strange. I tried to do anything but paint. It was a very gradual process. I suppose I didn't mind getting kicked. I began to relish it. Terrible insults. I have always been ignored or insulted but it has been water off a duck's back.

'People won't accept me because I use a palette knife. It's all right to cut a sheep in half but a palette knife is out. You can use your nose or a toothbrush, but never a palette knife.

But I have never bothered about rules. I use one because I like the sheer thickness of paint, the sensuality of it. I think I spend most of my money on paint. Now I find that though my palette hasn't greatly altered, I am using a lot of slate white, which in oil painting is the equivalent of water. I am not a colourist. A colourist is like a juggler. He throws ten different colours in the air. I can only juggle with three. I learnt to paint with a fairly restricted palette and there is a sort of rhetoric in my work which is best translated into fewer colours.

'For me, painting has always been a matter of instinct. In your subconscious you know what you are doing. But the more it comes from the head, the less likely you are to be able to communicate its meaning. I love certain things and I am able to communicate them. Contemporary art tends to be pretentious and communicates itself to pretentious people.

'I don't want to have exhibitions now that I have had so many. I don't want to sell pictures. I hate continually painting pictures which go out of my studio straight away. I want to look at them.'

The Thackeray in Kensington wanted to stage a Millennium exhibition but Kyffin was against it. 'I want to send my best work to the Royal Academy,' he said. 'I don't think the RA will last. They are letting in so many people who cannot draw. When drawing comes back they won't know how to teach it. They will be left high and dry.

'Drawing will come back. People are bound to love the world around them and the only way you can show appreciation is by putting it down. If you are not equipped to put it down there is nothing else to do but sheep in formaldehyde.'

Kyffin was always dismissive of his own work, too. When he was 58 he told a critic: 'At my age artists don't improve. All I hope is that I don't get any worse.'

The most scholarly study of Kyffin's work has been done by Professor Alistair Crawford, the founder and former head of the School of Art at the University of Wales,

Aberystwyth. Himself a successful artist, photographer and printmaker, his work is in private collections all over the world.

He was a student at the Glasgow School of Art when he was seventeen. He remembered how impressed he had been by an article by Kyffin in *The Studio,* and arrived at the school full of Kyffin's words and carrying a palette knife, only to be warned what an evil influence Kyffin Williams was. For good measure, he was told the palette knife was an abomination. He ignored both warnings.

Crawford continued to hold Kyffin in high regard and, for his retrospective landscape exhibition in 1995, he contributed an appreciation of an artist he confessed had been a great influence, an artist he persuasively compared to Van Gogh. He wrote:

> 'There is no doubt that in the post-war period Kyffin Williams is the highest regarded and most successful living Welsh artist in Wales, in terms of both recognition and sales. That is by the public, not the art establishment...
>
> ...Kyffin played a role both in London and Wales as a traditionalist who put representation before abstraction, certainly emotion and passion before intellect and the public before the critic. In effect he championed the Expressionist and Romantic over the Conceptualist, but his main concern was not so much against Modern Art as a plea to maintain the value of tradition...
>
> Many feel that Kyffin's depiction of the landscape of Wales embodies the spirit of the place more than any other contemporary artist... If John Piper 'invented' the Welsh chapel, Kyffin invented the farmhouse and the drystone wall... Kyffin's landscape is as sparse as a

memory from childhood, run and re-run in the mind as if it was continually trying to find the answer to a riddle. His landscapes become a metaphor for the Welsh land just as his portraits are a metaphor for the Welsh people...

The artist that Kyffin is clearly closest to, and can most be identified with, is Van Gogh, who is probably his real mentor. Stylistically this can best be seen in the similarity of his drawing, which is often conducted in a similar manner to Van Gogh...

...comparison is really to be found in the similarity of the psychological state. Both work with a similar intensity and pace. Both were epileptic... there are great similarities not least in their sensual delight in impasto where paint itself becomes the object of desire. Both artists suffer from the knowledge that intense emotion brings in its wake despair. The despair of failure as an artist. Both take on the landscape and wrestle with it as if one were an angel and the other a devil. Both know that in their relation and reaction to landscape lies their own personality.'

Not surprisingly, the photographer Nicholas Sinclair, the son of Kyffin's much loved Rosalie and his godson, is an aficionado.

'He was the first artist I photographed for a book I planned on British artists,' he said. 'He was incredibly supportive. The use of the palette knife makes his work uniquely identifiable. Imitations never quite pull it off. His work has grown steadily. Very often artists peak and slowly decline as they get older. I think he produced his best work in his last ten years, the strongest work he has done, and particularly the seascapes. The late seascapes are like large abstracts.

'The portrait book was my idea. I came up on the last

day of the exhibition and told him it was madness to have assembled this collection of portraits and not to turn it into a book. He said nothing but when I got home there was a message on my answer phone which said turn right round and come back because you have to photograph the portraits. The Welsh Arts Council were coming to collect the paintings in three days so we had three very hectic days photographing pictures.

'I felt there should be a landscape book which should have come out twenty-five years ago. I wrote the introduction, helped in the selection and did all the photographs. We used a fragment of his output. There is enough for four more books.

'My mother bought the first picture he sold. It was a small landscape, and now her house is full of them. My christening present was a painting of a nun. So I have had his paintings around me literally since birth.

'He underrates his drawings, partly because they come so easily. He is a wonderful cartoonist because he is so spontaneous – and an unconventional draughtsman. I think it is important his talent is more widely recognised. His path through life has been exceptional. Knowing right from the word go that the Welsh landscape was his subject, he was committed to it. He is the only Welsh artist of the twentieth century of whom this can be said. In London, he must have been a fish out of water. Living in rented rooms must have been hell for him. The move back to Anglesey was very important.

'He had an exceptional knowledge of art history and the contemporary scene. It was tempting to think of him as tucked away in Anglesey but he knew exactly what was going on in the art world and in London. You could ask him about any artist, period or contemporary, and he knew exactly what they had done or were doing. He may not have approved of it, but he knew about contemporary art, so argued from the standpoint of knowledge.

'The Welsh art establishment likes to have a parental role. To take up new young artists and guide them and support them. Kyffin didn't need that. He has always sold. He had an incredibly loyal following. So in a way, the Arts Council did not matter to his career and I think they might have found that difficult to handle.'

Chapter eleven

In the final decades of his life Kyffin threw himself into the cultural cauldron that is the arts in Wales. Never with more enthusiasm than in the bizarre affair of the Tunnicliffe Bequest, with Anglesey Borough Council as an unlikely Medici.

Charles Tunnicliffe was born in 1901, a Cheshire farmer's son who studied etchings, engraving and fine art at the Royal College of Art. In the 1920s he illustrated, with incomparable wood engravings, Henry Williamson's classic books *Tarka the Otter* and *Salar the Salmon*. By the 1930s he had become an ardent bird watcher. He moved to Anglesey in 1947 and made his home at Malltraeth, on the estuary of the river Cefni, which teems with bird life. Kyffin was a frequent visitor to 'Shorelands', Tunnicliffe's bungalow on the beach, and the two became friends. Both men were RAs but their rivalry, if it existed at all, was never obvious. They were lavish in their praise of each other's work.

Tunnicliffe was the more famous of the two outside Wales and in the mid-1970s David Robinson, the editorial director of the publishers Gollancz, came up from London to discuss a biography. In Tunnicliffe's studio he spotted a dusty album. Looking idly through it, he saw it was a collection of meticulously drawn birds. Tunnicliffe told him it was a collection of measured drawings he had done of dead birds, which he had started when his wife brought home a wild duck for supper.

'I measured things like wingspan and made plumage

sketches, studies of bone structure and so on. They are not meant for exhibition. I use them to help me get the birds in my paintings right,' he explained.

Very much against his will, Tunnicliffe agreed to let Gollancz publish these drawings as a taster to the biography which country author Ian Niall was writing. The biography sold well enough, but 90,000 copies of the *Sketchbook of Birds* were sold pre-publication. Although in Bangor, if proof were needed about prophets in their own country, it was remaindered.

Tunnicliffe died in 1979 before the book came out. Among his papers his executors found two other books, his *Shorelands Winter Diary* and *Shorelands Summer Diary*, both of which were published to a rapturous reception. His works and his royalties went to his sister Dolly but, under pressure, she divided everything between his eleven nephews and nieces. Somewhere along the way his dying wish that his collection should be kept together at the Royal Academy was forgotten.

In May 1981, John Smith, an Anglesey fitter with an interest in art, saw that Tunnicliffe's paintings, including the measured drawings that he never wished to be on public show, were being auctioned at Christie's. He had been a friend of Tunnicliffe and, concerned, he contacted the leader of Anglesey Council, Elwyn Schofield, as a matter of urgency.

Smith recalled: 'Councils are criticised for being slow to move but Anglesey Council moved quickly on this one and I will always be grateful to the local authority for this. I did everything through my local councillors and it was a delight to see the democratic process working for good.'

The council's chief executive worked overtime to clinch

a deal with the family in the week before the auction. His efforts were successful. For £400,000 the council became owners of the Tunnicliffe collection. There was a snag. The purchase price did not include the copyright, which might have been expected to have been part of the deal. Copyright on their uncle's work was retained by the family, which meant that only they, and not the council, would have the right to reproduce or franchise the paintings. Thus a very lucrative market that might have recovered the purchase price was lost to Anglesey. In fairness to the councillors, it might have seemed less important to them at the time than keeping the paintings in their original home.

Unlike most other rural councils, Anglesey's coffers were brimming over. The closure of the Suez Canal in 1956 meant that, in common with other oil companies, Shell's oil tankers had to make a costly and time-consuming voyage round the Horn to their refineries. The answer was to build giant tankers, but that brought its own problems. Shell's tankers were now too big to sail up to its oil refinery at Ellesmere Port. Merseyside councils refused the company's offer to build an offshore terminal so they turned to Anglesey. At a series of lunches and presentations, Shell offered handsome royalties if the island council would let them build an offshore terminal and a pumping station at Rhosgoch, in the north of the island near Amlwch. Through this terminal, the company proposed to transport crude oil to Ellesmere Port via 26 miles of underground pipes. It would convey a 25 million gallon load. It was a dazzling piece of engineering, and over a period of eleven years would bring Anglesey an income of £6,500,000.

Anglesey gratefully accepted the deal despite a storm of

protest from conservationists. In the event, the Suez Canal soon re-opened so only limited use was made of the facility and its load never exceeded ten million gallons. But there was never a single case of oil spillage and Anglesey was rich, though perhaps not beyond the dreams of avarice.

For a hidden agenda lurked behind the council's decision to buy the Tunnicliffe collection. Its offices were housed in a ramshackle series of huts and prefabricated buildings surrounding the main headquarters. An inner cabinet met and decided that a gallery to house the collection should be incorporated in a larger scheme that would include council offices, courts and county council buildings. The gallery itself would cost £300,000 a year to run and need a staff of seven.

A contact in the council told me about the scheme and I wrote a story for the *Sunday Mirror*, which included criticisms from other councillors. When the plan of the inner cabinet for a three-phase building programme at a total cost of £8 million was presented to the council, it was thrown out.

Kyffin had been delighted when the council bought the Tunnicliffe collection but dismayed when he read of the plan. He hurried to offer an alternative suggestion. Shorelands, Tunnicliffe's home, had been bought by a couple who found it inconvenient. They were ready to sell for £90,000. Part of the bungalow could be used to house the collection and the other part made into a flat for a 'resident bird artist' who would act as guardian.

His was one of twenty-five inexpensive alternatives ranging from Llanfairpwll station to Presaddfed, a mansion at Bodedern with a Gertrude Jekyll garden. None was accepted.

At about this time, Anglesey was visited by Shell UK's managing director, who informed the council that the agreement would last only until 1988 and the company could not go on making annual payments of £600,000. The council was undeterred. A suggestion was made to the effect that if there was not enough revenue from oil to maintain the gallery, then a merchant bank should be approached for a loan.

Kyffin led a protest movement that included 25 local and cash-starved Anglesey community councils. For eight years the arguments went on and for several of those years the Tunnicliffe collection of paintings and drawings languished in a cellar at the National Gallery in Cardiff. It looked as though there would never be a place to house it (although, curiously, a director was appointed for the non-existent gallery).

Four years after the paintings were bought, and another four years before a much more modest gallery was opened at Llangefni, Denise Black (later Morris), an award winning curator from Scunthorpe, was head-hunted. It proved a brilliant choice. From the moment it opened in 1998, Oriel Ynys Môn was an outstanding success under her inspired leadership.

She and Kyffin quickly became allies. He worked tirelessly for the cause. In 1990 he donated 293 drawings, including the copyright, to the gallery. Even then, they were estimated to be worth well over £10,000 and their value has increased handsomely since.

Under Mrs Morris's guidance the gallery won a clutch of awards and put on exhibitions by local artists which gave it the best attendance figures in North Wales and among the best in the whole of the principality. Alas, she got little support from the council. When under yet another local government reorganisation Anglesey became a county authority, her application for the post of director of leisure was turned down. It went instead to Elspeth Mitcheson, the former director of leisure for Gwynedd. By 1998 relations between the two women had become so bad that Denise felt she could no longer work there. The council accepted her resignation with no show of regret.

Kyffin was incensed. From that day onwards he refused to visit the gallery and cancelled plans to have his 80th birthday retrospective exhibition there. When at the end of the year Denise took the council to an industrial tribunal with a claim for wrongful dismissal (which she lost), Kyffin paid her considerable legal fees from the proceeds of a collection he had done of judicial caricatures. Such quiet acts of kindness were typical of him.

In the same year, 1998, a Kyffin painting was shown on the *Antiques Road Show*. It was valued at £15,000 by the expert Rupert Maas who told its delighted owner: 'The market must in years to come recognise Kyffin Williams as an important artist. There is something about him that captures exactly the colours and tones of his country. This painting contains many different shades of the same colour. It ranges from khaki, through slate grey to brilliant green. I like particularly the slabby painting technique and the greys of the slate slabs. It is all caught marvellously. He shares with Constable the ability to catch a landscape.'

Also in 1998, a painting of a Welsh Black bull, owned by O G Thomas, the president of the Royal Welsh Show, was auctioned at the show for £7,000. In the following year, a set of 150 signed prints of an Anglesey cottage, which he donated to the National Eisteddfod to commemorate its visit to Anglesey, raised £12,000 for Eisteddfod funds.

What pleased him most, though, was the support he got from a powerful figure in the British establishment, Lord Emlyn Hooson QC. At the launch of his lavishly illustrated book, *The Land & the Sea,* at the National Library of Wales, Lord Hooson, said that Kyffin was one of the most outstanding artists to emerge in Wales over the last half century. He went on:

> He is an uncompromising man, finds little to his taste in the dictates of either mediocrity or the establishment and he has made it his business to improve the institutional situation in terms of professionalism and the status of Welsh work in Wales. His complete independence, both in his painting and his various battles with institutions, has led to a different view of art being taken and has contributed greatly to the more favourable environment in which, gradually, younger artists are able to work in Wales.
>
> No man was ever truer to himself than Kyffin. It is this engaging individualism that so endears him to the people of Wales and enables him to relate to them and they to him in a way few poets or musicians even have been able to achieve.

He compared his skills of communication with those of Wales's most revered hymn writers and poets.

> Every now and then Wales throws up somebody who in his or her way and in a particular art form communicates with the nation. William Williams Pantycelyn was one, Dafydd ap Gwyllim was another, Ann Griffiths another. It would not surprise me that in

the future, as for so many of us now, Kyffin is able, like them, to communicate with the inner soul of Wales.

Let me conclude by saying the launch of this book enables us to acknowledge our great appreciation first of all of Kyffin, the man – his indomitable spirit, his enhancement of our appreciation of our country, of our people and of our idiosyncrasies. We also salute him as a truly Welsh artist with an international appeal and possibly, by establishments, more appreciated outside Wales than in. But an artist to whom the people of Wales relate.

No Welshman, surely, had a better epitaph.

Epilogue

Kyffin was the oddest invalid I ever met. Though genuinely suffering from a multiplicity of ailments, he nonetheless managed to hunt with the Snowdon pack, drive endless distances without any evidence of tiredness, walk miles and climb mountains I could only watch through half-closed fingers. He was impervious to cold. Indeed, when he was painting, he was impervious to anything.

Inevitably the years took their toll and by his eighties he was beginning to flag. I moved from Wales, so for two years I did not see him. I loved Anglesey so much and missed it so badly I could not bear to go back, though we kept in touch by phone and letter.

When eventually I did steel myself and returned to Llanfairpwll to stay with his neighbours and friends, the Reverend Peter Gledhill and his wife Bridget, Kyffin came to dinner clutching a lovingly inscribed book of his portraits.

I was shocked when I saw him. For the first time he looked old and unwell. His spirit, though, was unaffected. That evening he sparkled with outrageous anecdotes and hurled verbal thunderbolts at 'Britart', art schools and painters who could not draw. Peter was a scholarly man, whom we both loved dearly, and Kyffin and I had a private game to see who could be the first with an outrageous remark to make him rub his head and say, with great gravity, 'I am afraid I cannot quite agree with that.'

Kyffin was the ideal dinner guest.

He could even make R S Thomas laugh.

We had another private joke. I told him he was kept alive by the chicken casseroles which coursed through his veins, the product of a convoy of local ladies who brought delicious dishes down the pitted lane to his house by the sea, concerned he wasn't getting enough to eat. Enough? He dined out most nights, once a week with us, once with the Marquess and Marchioness of Anglesey and weekends would find him being pampered to death by Annwen and Bengy Carey-Evans at their home in Criccieth. He may have been Wales's greatest painter – I am biased and, anyway, not competent to judge – but he was certainly Wales's most loved man.

When I returned to the scenery-free Fens, the letters and the phone calls continued but they were not as frequent.

When his *Kyffin in Venice* book came out, my wife Celia bought it for my birthday in May. Kyffin and I were both born on Ascension Day. Kyffin insisted this entitled us to two birthdays. She wrote to Kyffin to ask for a letter to paste in the front.

When the reply came, it was written by Denise Morris, the woman whose professionalism and enthusiasm had initiated the success of Oriel Ynys Môn and a constant friend and carer to Kyffin whom she revered.

The letter read:

> Dear Celia,
> I am fully conscious of the proximity of the birthday of Ian and myself but I am afraid I am unable to mark the auspicious date by writing a suitable inscription. The reason for this is that I can no longer write, even though I am able to draw a bit somehow. Strange, but there we are.

Denise is writing this for me, as she does for all those who get in touch with me. I am very lucky.

Do let me know if you are coming down here again. I always enjoy seeing you.

Love,

Kyffin

(dictated to Denise)

Denise had added a note: 'Kyffin is very weak and tires quickly. He could hardly raise the breath to dictate this letter, but I am hoping he will be stronger soon.'

Alarmed, I wrote at once, and this reply came:

Dear Ian,

I was very touched to get your letter. My battle with bogey goes on. The medical people are very kind and they are pulling out all the stops. I am also grateful to all my friends round here who cannot seem to do enough for me.

I am so glad you are settling down in March. It must have been difficult for you – just as I couldn't leave here.

As for the Buddhism, I am delighted to think it is helping you. It has always been very attractive to Welsh people and there have been a lot of well-known Buddhists. I could have been a Buddhist, I think, as I could well have been a vegetarian.

It was good to hear from you and Celia. We must keep in touch.

Love,

Kyffin

Again Denise had added a note: 'Kyffin is getting very weak but is in good enough spirits as you can see by his letter. His oncologist has put in for a new drug for him so we are all trying for optimism.'

Soon after, came the phone call we had dreaded. It was from another friend, Father Brian Jones who, with Dr Margaret Wood, had frequently entertained Kyffin to some of Margaret's epicurean meals at their cottage in Llansadwrn, a cottage that Kyffin had painted in his youth. The picture now hangs on their wall.

Kyffin once described himself as 'an obsessive, depressive, diabetic epileptic'. Some years ago, prostate cancer (and later lung cancer) joined the enemy fighting for his body. Kyffin reacted with wry humour. He was treated by the legendary consultant Miss Evans at Bodelwyddan Hospital, a lady, he told me, who had seen every notable backside (and private parts) in Wales. She was the recipient of some of his finest cartoons and poems.

In August 2006, the cancer had him on the ropes. He was taken to Ysbyty Gwynedd and two weeks later transferred to St Tysilio Nursing Home, less than a mile from his home on the Straits, where on Friday, September 1, he died.

The Marquess of Anglesey told me that the day he died, Kyffin, to everyone's surprise, ate a hearty breakfast of bacon and eggs.

On Monday, September 11, the man who expected a quiet funeral in a country church had what amounted in Wales to a state funeral, conducted by another friend, the Archbishop of Wales, Dr Barry Morgan.

The Prince of Wales, who had invited Kyffin to Highgrove to show him his paintings, was represented by the Lord Lieutenant of Gwynedd, Huw Daniel.

The coffin was draped with white roses and dark red carnations, and six hundred people, most of whom knew and loved him, packed Bangor Cathedral for the hour-long service of thanksgiving for his life and work.

His godson Nicholas Sinclair paid a tribute to the man who thought of him as the son he never had; a second tribute came from Professor Derec Llwyd Morgan, the former principal of Aberystwyth University. The lesson was read by the Marquess and a favourite psalm by Father Brian Jones, a Catholic priest.

It came as no surprise that Kyffin had planned his own service to the last ecumenical detail. It was his final work of art. Bryn Terfel sang one of Kyffin's best-loved songs *My Little Welsh Home*, accompanied by harpist Elinor Bennett.

Ynys Môn AM Ieuan Wyn Jones commented: 'It was absolutely amazing, absolutely wonderful. We had one great artist singing to another.'

Professor Morgan, who comes from Anglesey, is chairman of the Kyffin Williams Trust that was set up to plan the gallery within a gallery at Oriel Ynys Mon, Llangefni, dedicated to Kyffin's work. In his tribute he explained the one luxury that Kyffin permitted himself, a Volvo motorcar.

Kyffin had called in at his local Volvo dealers to pick up his morning newspaper. A girl in the sale-room told him she had just the car for him with a YSK registration. She said it stood for 'Young Sir Kyffin'. He bought it on the spot.

The Archbishop, a former bishop of Bangor, said that the fact the cathedral was full of people from all walks of society was testimony to the esteem in which Kyffin was held – not just as an artist, but as a man.

'We have come out of respect and to give thanks for him. But we are only able to do so because he, in the end, consented to have a service such as this. His preferred option was a quiet burial at Llanfairynghornwy. A quiet burial because he himself was self deprecating about his work. *Not much talent really*, he once said.'

In the end, as he always did, Kyffin got his way. He was buried in the tiny churchyard at Llanfairynghornwy. He would have been amazed, outwardly horrified, but secretly pleased, by the explosion of tributes that followed his death.

The *Daily Telegraph* obituarist wrote:

> Sir Kyffin Williams, who died yesterday aged 88, was one of the great figures of Welsh art in the second half of the 20th century.
>
> His paintings of the North Wales landscape and the people who lived and worked there were executed in a bold and idiosyncratic palette-knife style, and became enduring and instantly recognisable images; meanwhile, his unselfish and energetic contributions to the artistic life of Wales did much to enhance its sense of distinctive cultural identity.

Betsan Powys, at that time arts and media correspondent for BBC Wales, recalled that Kyffin said he spent a lifetime responding to the landscape and the people of the area in which he grew up. In a 1999 BBC interview she recalled him saying: 'I sometimes feel the last canvas I have covered is the last canvas I will ever cover, but then I go and paint another one and so it goes on.'

The Times obituary headline ran: 'Painter who celebrated the landscapes and people of his beloved North Wales with passion and humour.' It continued: 'Sir Kyffin Williams was a portraitist, a painter of North Welsh landscapes and seascapes, and an amused chronicler of his own and other people's foibles.

'Rain-lashed, green-grey landscapes, stormy, slate-grey seascapes and weather-beaten, pink-grey farmers are the recurring themes of Williams's art, sketched and, in many cases, painted outdoors in his beloved North Wales.'

In the *Daily Post*, the regional newspaper, David Greenwood wrote: 'The 88-year-old Anglesey born painter, regarded by many as Wales's greatest ever artist, died at the St Tysilio Nursing Home at 11.30am. He had been at the home on the outskirts of Llanfairpwll for just over a week after spending two weeks as a patient at Ysbyty Gwynedd, Bangor. He had been suffering from lung and prostate cancer.

'Last night Sally Goddard, an executor of his estate, described Sir Kyffin, who never married, as a "great friend"... "I had known him for 28 years and we liked walking the Welsh countryside together, particularly across North Wales. He was a lovely man and superb company," said Ms Goddard, who lives in Garth, Bangor. "Because of his illness he hadn't done so much work over the last year or so."

'Sir Kyffin's death comes as major efforts were being stepped up to build a "gallery within a gallery" at Oriel Ynys Môn to house his works.

'Sir Kyffin, who lived and had his studio at Llanfairpwll overlooking the Menai Strait, had even backed a major fund-raising by promoting the sale of signed prints of his work.

'Vicky MacDonald, curator of the Royal Cambrian Academy, who worked with Sir Kyffin when he was president for 12 years, last night described him as charismatic. She said: "What can you say about one of Wales's greatest ever artists? A private view would light up when he walked in. People would be enthralled just talking and listening to him. As a person he was a delight, so kind and gentle, but not afraid to speak his mind"…'

Author and broadcaster David Meredith, also writing in the *Daily Post*, said: 'Kyffin Williams, Sir Kyffin or, as he preferred, just Kyffin, was without question for me Wales's greatest artist, an artistic giant undertaking his chosen profession of "making a living by painting" with determination, perseverance and discipline.

'Kyffin believed in passion, love and obsession as being vital to good art and that obsession – "something deep down" – was more important than talent even. He certainly imbued all his painting with love, his love of the mountains of Gwynedd, and the sea as it crashed on the shores of his native Anglesey.'

In the *Western Mail*, Tryst Williams wrote: 'His artistic legacy continued to be reaffirmed, cementing his place as one of Wales's best-loved painters. His works were yesterday expected to rocket in value over the coming weeks.

'Former Young Artist of the Year Dan Llywelyn Hall was one of many artists to pay generous tribute to the Anglesey-born painter who died on Friday, aged 88. He said, "No single artist has touched on the Welsh psyche as profoundly as Kyffin Williams. His art has helped to shape and define the nation's visual identity. He touched on the melancholy of the landscape and the contradiction of the exhilaration and isolation that we can sometimes experience. As an artist, I admired his dedication to his subject matter and his tireless efforts to promote Welsh art to an international audience – like few have before him. His palette of colour was distinctly Welsh and he somehow managed to describe the landscape in the most succinct and economical of ways. For me, his portraits probed even deeper exposing human struggle and adding a certain grit to his subjects.

"I wrote to Kyffin on many occasions sending samples of recent work including a portrait I'd not long ago completed of Cliff Morgan. He always responded with insightful comments and suggestions of how to progress. He often helped to describe the difficulties faced whilst living as an artist and how he'd overcome them in his lifetime".'

Tryst Williams wrote that the internet auction site eBay received a flurry of bids in the wake of Kyffin's death. 'One vendor was even offering a copy of Saturday's *Western Mail,* featuring news of Sir Kyffin's death, for sale at £8.99.'

His article continued: 'Meanwhile Wales's richest artist called on the Assembly to help save Sir Kyffin's work for the nation. Andrew Vicari, who was official painter for the Saudi Arabian government, said a permanent exhibition of his art should be put on display immediately. The pair were long-time friends and were due to paint each others' portraits next year.

'Vicari said, "Kyffin was one of nature's greatest gentlemen – a great artist and a great friend. I hope that Wales, for once, tries to do something marvellous to commemorate the superb work of one of its most famous, and favourite, sons. There are statues to great sportsmen, museums dedicated to ancient artefacts, but the majority of the nation's art treasures are stored away where nobody can see them. I would urge the Assembly to find some way to purchase for the nation as many of Kyffin's treasures as possible."

'Ironically, during his lifetime, Sir Kyffin had himself campaigned tirelessly for a Welsh National Art Gallery to be set up.'

#